# OUR FAIR SHARE

How One Small Change
Can Create a More Equitable
American Economy

## BRIAN C. JOHNSON

Broadleaf Books
Minneapolis

OUR FAIR SHARE
How One Small Change Can Create a More Equitable American Economy

Graphs appearing in chapters 6 and 7 are adapted from *The Spirit Level: Why Greater Equality Makes Societies Stronger* by Richard Wilkinson and Kate Pickett, copyright © 2009, 2010 by Richard Wilkinson and Kate Pickett. Used by permission of The Equality Trust.

Cover image: iStock photography
Cover design: 1517 Media

Print ISBN: 978-1-5064-7075-7
eBook ISBN: 978-1-5064-7076-4

*To my parents,*
*who taught me that America's greatest beauty*
*lies in our people and our ideals*

# CONTENTS

# CONTENTS

# 1

# OUT OF MANY, ONE

We may have democracy, or we may have wealth concentrated in the hands of a few, but we can't have both.

—Justice Louis Brandeis

We have a story in my family, and like all family stories, it is probably mostly true and a little bit not. My sister, who is two years younger than I am, has always been able to charm a stranger. When she was four years old, she used to go around telling adults how old she was with the accent of a New York cabbie. But when she turned five, she proudly announced her age with the lilt of a southern debutante.

Like all good family stories, this tale reflects both our roots and our trajectory. My parents hail from New York City. My dad grew up in Queens. My mom's family is from the Bronx, and she was raised out on Long Island. But early on, each of my folks' lives led them out of New York. Soon, two New Yorkers whose families had lived in New York since they immigrated to America in the late nineteenth century had two children born in Kentucky.

If you were to meet my parents today, you would be hard-pressed to detect a New York accent. But as I was growing up, my mom in particular had a pronounced one, and my early patterns of speech reflected where my parents came from. But over the two decades of my childhood, we were nomads. In fact, by the time I had turned fourteen, I had lived in eleven different homes, in nine different towns, in five different states, and even in two different countries. So at four, my sister living in Monterey Bay, California, spoke like her New York parents. But by five, when she was living in eastern North Carolina, she spoke like her southern kindergarten classmates. We talked like we lived, carrying our roots and growing with every new community.

But beyond speech, this nomadic existence deeply influenced the way I learned to approach communities more broadly. After each move, I had to figure out how to integrate into the ever-changing, motley cast of people around me. I studied what they talked about, what they valued, and how they spent their time. To be honest, I stumbled frequently and often stood on the outside of new communities for long uncomfortable periods. But this work at integration had its own prize.

Like a blacksmith hammering out a new scythe, this regular beating of newness and outsiderness developed in me a hard-forged tool for being in the world. The core of that tool was a deep understanding that each community viewed itself as good in its own right. That the way it saw the world around it and its relationship to that world was largely decent. That theirs was a culture of beauty and virtue. When I approached each new community with an assumption of its own goodness, the community readily shared that goodness.

I used this tool repeatedly as I got older. As I approached new places, I sought first to understand. By honoring the worldview each community held, I could begin building meaningful relationships with its members. When I graduated from my middle-class public schools to the courtyards of intergenerational privilege at Princeton,

When I ate lunch in the teachers' lounge in a Baton Rouge elementary school. When I stood in front of assemblies of two hundred parents at the public schools I ran in central Los Angeles. When I sat down across from LGBTQ people at coffee shops in Peoria. This tool embedded itself deep in my psyche and in my approach over these years.

Most fundamentally, using this tool has taught me how woven together we all are in this country: CEOs and senators at Princeton, Black parents in Baton Rouge, immigrant families in Los Angeles, trans men and women in central Illinois. Over nearly four decades of moving and working around our country, I've learned that what underlies America's greatness is our commonness and our connectedness.

## Commonness and Connectedness:
## What Binds Us Together and Makes Us Uniquely American

For most of the first half of my career, I worked with and on behalf of low-income families of color. We fought together to make sure their schools delivered on America's promise: that regardless of race or class or zip code, their children would be given an equal shot at opportunity. And then in 2009, in my early thirties, I accepted an offer to run a racially and socioeconomically diverse public school in the heart of Hollywood. Here was a community that was among the most diverse in America, and our school reflected that. We had children of Oscar and Emmy nominees, television network presidents, and talent agents going to school with the children of immigrants whose parents didn't speak English. We held these communities in almost equal measure. Our student population was nearly half white and half children of color. Half of our students came from low-income families and half came from middle- and upper-income families.

Going into this work, I thought that my interactions with privileged families were going to be wildly different from those I had with low-income ones. While these two groups differed on the margins—and mostly in how they approached me and school leadership—their hopes and dreams were largely similar. Both sets of families cared most about whether their children were safe and loved. They focused on whether their children's unique potential for genius was sought out, valued, and developed.

As I got to know these families better, I learned that it wasn't just how they approached their children's schooling that bound them in similarity, but so much more. I can honestly say, after having worked with thousands of families over nearly two decades, that I have never met a parent who didn't want better for their kid than they had. And nearly all were working hard—most in highly productive ways, a few in dysfunctional ways—to give their child this opportunity.

This is what I mean by *commonness*. Regardless of race, class, ethnicity, profession, country of origin, native language, or religion, these parents were engaged in a shared struggle to make the lives of their children good and safe and vibrant.

I don't mean to suggest some Pollyannaish view of the world here. Differences existed—meaningful ones. Some parents expected their children to be compliant. Others raised them to question authority. Some parents wanted limited academic expectations set for their children, while others preferred rigorous ones. Some viewed our teachers as contract employees who were expected to deliver a service the parents paid for with their taxes. Others viewed teachers as largely unassailable experts.

Differences exist in our country as well, meaningful ones. Even throughout the span of my life and among the people I have gotten to know, these differences stand out in stark relief: My Princeton classmate who grew up as an only child of wealthy New York parents. The single Black mother raising three children and working part-time as a teacher's aide in Baton Rouge. The vibrant Latina teacher who graduated from Harvard and taught in the East Los Angeles neighborhood of her childhood. The young gay man coming of age in the southern tip of Illinois. The differences in these people—in their struggles, in their worldviews, in their political ideology, and even in some of their values—are real. But in looking at these differences, commonness often unveils itself.

Writer Anne Lamott shares that "when we study the differences, we see in bolder relief what we have in common."[1] Because at the heart of differences beats the same questions: Will my family be safe and secure? Will my neighbors respect me and treat me fairly? Will I be valued? Will my work have meaning? Can I provide for my family? Will my child have a better life than I do?

But beyond sharing commonness, we are also bound together. A friend of mine works actively for justice in schools both in New York and across the country. One night over dinner, I asked him more about why he did this work. In language that didn't surprise me, he spoke movingly about his daughters. He talked about how he wanted a better world for them. Then he told me about his community and how deeply he wanted the same success for the children on his block that he wanted for his own daughters. He asked, "What if the cure for cancer is locked up in the mind of the little Latino boy that will never get out because we have not given that child the opportunities he deserved and needed?"

That's the crux of it all.

Our destinies are bound together. The doctor who might save my husband's life in the future may be in medical school on the South Side of Chicago right now. The teacher who might inspire my daughter may be in college in St. Louis today.

Undoubtedly these themes of commonness and connected-ness matter on a human scale. But in America, they form together to create the civic fabric of our shared identity. To be connected and share commonness across lines of difference is the heart of our national identity. This bond across differences is not just our history; it is who we are.

When Martin Luther King Jr. reminded us that "we are caught in an inescapable network of mutuality, tied in a single garment of destiny," he was surely speaking to us as people, but he was more importantly speaking to us as Americans.[2]

Our history teaches us this. We have no single founding point. We were always many: the Puritans of Massachusetts seeking a place to build out their religious experiment, the second sons of second sons fleeing to Virginia to live out the gentry heritage denied them in England, the Catholic Calverts and their religious com-patriots seeking to carve out a safehold in Maryland, free from the chaos of on-again, off-again persecution at home. At a minimum, we had thirteen foundings.

But probably closer to the truth is that every time a foot set down on this soil for the first time, we had another founding. That includes the shackled feet first touching land after being criminally stowed away on slavers' ships. And all these foundings followed the foundings of thousands of years before, when the first human feet crested the Appalachian Mountains from the west and, finding the sea, ended an eastern march of thousands of years.

E pluribus unum.

Out of many, one.

Our original motto as a nation.

America's emergence is one of the great experiments in human history. Nearly 250 years ago, our forefathers and foremothers wagered that we could build a nation not on shared history or exclusive racial heritage but on common values. That the landless heirs of Virginia and Catholic asylum seekers of Maryland and countless other groups could bind together across difference and geography to form something never created before in the history of the world. Our founders were far from perfect. They enslaved people, excluded women, and waged war on our country's Indigenous people. But in the chaos of their indignities, they built a framework that made America's promise unique in the world, and they gave later generations the tools to expand beyond their own limited ideas of who we could be as a people.

Our commonness and connectedness across our many differences is our shared national heritage: More so than Englishness (for there already was an England) or whiteness (for white nations existed already) or Christianness (for Christian countries and kingdoms had existed for centuries), e pluribus unum is what makes us American.

## We Are Under Assault by an Economic System That Denies Our Values

Our unique American experiment—that we are bound together by our shared values—is under siege in a new and dangerous way. It is under attack by a rapidly devolving economy that splits citizens into owners and workers, then aggregates returns almost exclusively to those owners.

From 1980 to 2014, median wages for individuals in America increased by 61 percent (controlling for inflation). But here is the kicker: for the bottom 50 percent of earners, there was almost no increase at all.[3] Think about it: from 1980 to the mid-2010s, the size of our economy nearly tripled[4] and the per-capita GDP nearly doubled,[5] but most Americans saw no real increase in their earnings.

We see this widening gap manifest itself all around us. The past four decades have brought about previously unthinkable economic progress. We have seen technological innovations revolutionize commerce. We have seen the reduction of trade barriers lead to the creation of a middle class in countries across the globe while better products become more available at cheaper prices here in America. We have seen an increasingly democratic and connected global market lead to a dramatic decline in wars and conflicts.

But the boon of all this progress has not been equally shared. Owners and top income earners have hoarded the benefits of our prosperity. Middle- and low-income Americans have borne the brunt of the pain that comes with massive growth and rapid transformation. While free trade agreements have made all our cars and computers and coffees better and cheaper, they have also shuttered entire factories and shaken whole towns. While e-commerce has sent us all to the internet for our shopping, it has led to a "retail meltdown" across our country.[6] As wages stagnate, everyday costs continue to rise. Housing, health care, and childcare eat up more of a household's budget today than they did fifty years ago. Economists Anne Case and Angus Deaton have found that since 1999, mortality rates for middle-aged white American men with a high school education or less have been on the rise, fueled by "deaths of despair." "Progressively worsening labor market opportunities . . . for whites with low levels of education," have brought about a spike in drug overdoses, suicide, and alcoholism.[7]

This rising inequality is a threat, as it would be to any democracy. But it poses a unique threat to America. It tears at our sense of common bonds. It denies our heritage that we are tied together. It contradicts our espoused national values, the best parts of our history, and our highest ideals, ultimately endangering our grand experiment.

The problem of rising inequality is that, like Mother Teresa says, we "have forgotten that we belong to each other."[8] In America, we have built an entire economic structure around the premise that we are not bound together but instead are independent actors whose relationships with one another are merely transactional. We have unpegged owners' wealth from workers' wealth. We have built a modern economy that rejects e pluribus unum.

An American economic system that ignores the fundamental truth of our connectedness by untethering its players from one another will eventually break down. This is not theoretical. The sense of common collective identity that undergirds our democracy is cracking all around us right now.

We saw hints of this breakdown with the rise of the Tea Party and the eventual election of Donald Trump to the US presidency. Fear and anger boil up when people experience no economic progress, limited prospects, and culminating despair. Someone must be at fault for this, many conclude. So when demagogues suggest that the cause of this plight is the enemy among us—when they peddle false narratives that a foreign-born president illegally occupies the White House, that unemployed grifters in the inner city cash in on "Obama phones" and free health insurance, that tree-hugging environmentalists protect birds over American jobs, or that the Mexicans and the Chinese steal American jobs and take them overseas—many in our country are ripe to accept these lies. In 2015, 34 percent of Americans believed Obama was an "imminent threat" to our country, more than those who believed that Russian president Vladimir Putin was.[9]

We've seen evidence of the fraying of our social fabric on the left as well. On the heels of the Great Recession, where millions suffered but no one went to jail, a flame of anticorporatism ignited and burned from Occupy Wall Street through the 2016 campaign to the Resistance. This central narrative is fueled by a belief that "the 1 percent" truly hate everyday Americans, and that corporate shareholders and CEOs are hell-bent on screwing over the lives of the middle class to enrich themselves. Nearly ten years after the crash that initiated the Great Recession, 59 percent of Americans still believed Wall Street was a threat to our economy.[10]

We cannot keep marching down this path for long before the cracks give way to a collapse of the entire system. I know of few societies in history where a widening gap between the ultrarich and everyone else bolstered a stable, healthy society.

When we only allow returns to flow to owners and top earners, the system incentivizes these owners and earners to hoard these returns jealously, to invest among themselves in stock options and dividends, and to spend it in the luxury economy. I do not say this ascribing any animus to owners or managers. Nobody wakes up every day saying they want to swindle the American middle and working classes—or at least nobody I know. It is the system that allows for this, that creates this, and that encourages this. It takes an incredible amount of contrarian willingness to make personal decisions that run counter to the system: to pay more in taxes than is required, to reject the compensation package to allow for higher wages down the corporate ladder, to return the dividend. Even if good and well-meaning individuals are willing to buck the entire system with their discrete choices, the impact on the system wouldn't be felt at all—a ripple on the shore of a nighttime lake.

## A Way Forward That Honors What We Own Together

But . . .

What if we created a system that wasn't at odds with our American values but consistent with them? What if that system recognized that what makes America great is that we aim to bind together our separate histories toward a common destiny? What if it reflected how our economy grows not simply at the hands of individuals but as a result of us all coming together?

To create such a system, we must first recognize that the value created by our economy is due, in significant part, to four types of wealth we all own jointly as Americans. Peter Barnes, in his ground-breaking work *With Liberty and Dividends for All*, lays out much of this foundation, which I build upon.

First are our natural resources—the land, the sun, the water, the minerals in the ground, and the wind in the sky. Our earth bestows these resources on each of us equally. We may assign possession and use them differently, but at the core, we share equal ownership in these.

Second are the societal resources we use together like our roads, our schools, our military, and our power grids. They are paid for out of our common taxes and are available for open use by all.

Third are the systems we have inherited from our ancestors. The primary one is our constitutional system that outlines the principle of a government directed by free citizens who come together to limit governmental overreach, maximize the common good, and protect the rights of individuals. But this is not the only system. We have financial systems and markets that allow for easy transfer of value, a patent system that spurs innovation, and legal systems that protect the rights of the individual from undue government coercion or mob rule. Those belong to all of us as well.

A fourth and final type of co-owned wealth is our collective willingness to accept and bind ourselves by the social contract that governs our nation. Laws exist to rein in individual rule-breakers, but collectively Americans agree to abide by a system of laws that respects property rights, protects our physical safety, and funds investments in the common good.

These four forms of wealth enable an ecosystem in which value can be created. Admittedly, these together are not sufficient to create value on their own. Individual innovation, talent, creativity, risk-taking, hard work, chutzpah, and good luck are all needed to create wealth. Our system is already built to acknowledge and reward an individual actor's contributions. But the system has failed to acknowledge that all those individual traits and actions would create no value if not enacted upon a foundation of our jointly owned assets. We have a system that has forgotten this. We have allowed a few individuals to use our collective wealth to create value and then hoard the returns.

What we need is a new structure to acknowledge that value is created using our jointly owned wealth. A country whose identity rests on the unique premise that we come together across our differences to create one common nation must distribute some of the returns made from commonly held wealth to their rightful owners.

We need a Citizen Dividend: 5 percent of all business profits in this country should be returned to the co-owners of the joint wealth used to create those profits. This is what a dividend is: a return of some fraction of profits to joint owners. As citizens who jointly own—each in equal measure—some of the wealth used to create those profits, we deserve an annual dividend from that co-owned wealth.

Individual owners should retain 95 percent of profits to pay in taxes and distribute as they see fit. Profits play a critical role in encouraging innovation, hard work, and measured risk-taking. But by requiring an annual 5 percent profit distribution as a Citizen Dividend, we would advance four additional social goods.

First, we would lighten the burden many families carry because of rising inequality. We would put cash directly into the hands of Americans who can use it to meet their greatest needs.

Second, when the shifts of our economy cause a major reaction—a factory closure, an industry disruption—we would ensure that those who are most harmed receive some benefit. By softening the blow of economic transformation, we would increase the likelihood that our society will retain the appetite for a rapidly evolving economy. A Citizen Dividend, paired with more targeted and robust policies, can play an important role in facilitating greater social acceptance of economic shifts.

Third, we would tie the individual well-being of each citizen to the collective well-being of our economy. We would ensure that we can no longer have an economic boom without everyone receiving some part of it. Beyond basic fairness, this connection would increase democratic will for progrowth policies that can further our economic advancement.

Finally, we would create a link among every individual in the economy. We are all tied to one another. When the immigrant's entrepreneurialism, the CEO's strategic decision-making, the shareholder's infusion of capital, and the worker's labor all play a role to increase business profits, all should benefit. We need one another. Through a Citizen Dividend, we would see a tangible return on one another's contributions. A Citizen Dividend would ensure that everyone benefits from economic growth, so everyone has a stake in the game. Rallying against "the 1 percent," or immigrant workers, or progrowth trade deals would negatively affect our individual pockets, not merely the abstract collective good.

### Making the Case for the Citizen Dividend

In our path together in this book, I will lead you through three stories, each building on the last.

First, I detail the rising economic inequality we currently face. I start by drawing heavily from economists such as Thomas Piketty, Emmanuel Saez, Gabriel Zucman, and Edward Wolff to explain how both income inequality and wage inequality have grown over the past forty years. To explore why inequality has accelerated so rapidly, I build off of an analysis from Nobel Prize–winning economist Angus Deaton.

Next, I illustrate how rising economic inequality is harmful to society. I detail the pains many Americans are feeling as essential costs rise but wages remain stagnant. I dive into Richard Wilkinson and Kate Pickett's research showing the host of negative social outcomes that are linked to rising inequality in rich countries. I explore how social mobility, social cohesion, and civic engagement have all suffered as inequality has increased. I conclude this section by drawing on the words of our founders and the experiences of early Americans to illuminate how this trend flies in the face of our deepest-held American values.

Finally, I articulate a vision for how we can use the Citizen Dividend to begin reducing inequality and tie our economy more firmly to our national values. I revisit more fully the nature of jointly owned wealth that private actors use to create value. I lay out the framework for the Citizen Dividend as a just way to compensate all Americans for the use of that wealth. I outline the benefits that might flow from such a dividend. Finally, I respond to some thoughtful questions this proposal undoubtedly raises, and I end by charting a path forward, offering ideas for how to bring about a Citizen Dividend.

Throughout, I will introduce you to a diverse array of Americans who are experiencing the injustices of rising economic inequality differently. You will meet a Catholic priest working as a labor leader, as well as a CEO of a health and wellness company, both of whom live in Chicago. You will come to know a parent activist from Houston and a political organizer and preacher in Harlem. You will learn about the lives of an immigrant rights activist who is raising her son in a predominantly white blue-collar town and about a mayoral candidate in Maine's second-largest city. Each of these figures gives us unique insight into how America's accelerated inequality is undermining the heart and soul of our country. Each gives form to our hope that we can redeem our nation by holding fast to our most central values.

Before moving on, it is best that I highlight a few things that this project is not.

First, this proposal is not a panacea for all our social or economic woes. A 5 percent dividend on business profits is a modest proposal—on its face and in its application. I do not suggest that putting this idea into practice will radically transform our way of being with one another all on its own. The Citizen Dividend is important mostly because it aligns our economy with our values. If one's values are good—and our national value of forging common identity across lines of difference is good—then we must align our practices more closely with our values. There will be concrete benefits from this alignment, but the primary purpose of the Citizen Dividend is not merely to realize those benefits. The primary purpose is to bring our practice and our values in closer harmony.

Second, there are many other proposals in the marketplace of ideas that aim to ambitiously tackle the challenge of rising inequality in America. Notable among them is the concept of a universal basic income (UBI), whereby everyone is granted the revenue needed to meet their needs. Work above that is therefore voluntary, disconnected from the provision of basic resources. UBI has gained some persuasive champions, like business leaders Mark Zuckerberg and Andy Stern. I do not present the concept of the Citizen Dividend to trump other ideas like a UBI, a sovereign wealth fund, or other forms of guaranteed income. In fact, the Citizen Dividend could be used in conjunction with those and other efforts to reduce inequality.

Third, I am not an academic. I am especially not an economist. I am a teacher, an organizer, and now the CEO of a civil rights organization. I have spent my career in classrooms, church basements, coffee shops, and people's living rooms. Others who read this with more storied academic backgrounds will undoubtedly have much to add to the proposal I outline here. I look forward to it.

### A Love Letter to Our Country

At its heart, this book is a love letter to our country. My grandmother passed away when I was fifteen. Before she died, she used to tell me a story about her uncle growing up in New York at the turn of the last century. Her German immigrant family arrived in the city poor, hopeful, and ready to work. But the family was growing, work was hard to find, and winter was brutal. So as a young boy, my great-uncle used to go to the railyards and taunt the workers mercilessly. When the workers had had enough, they threw coal at the boy to get him to run away. My great-uncle collected that coal and brought it home to heat the family house.

I don't know if the story is true; again, it is probably mostly true and a little bit not. But I do know that it captures something real about who my family is and who my grandmother believed us to be. We didn't come from much, but we were scrappy. And our scrappiness eventually paid off.

My grandmother had been a single mother raising two daughters in the 1960s on nothing but a high school education. Two generations later—two years after she died—I started my freshman year at Princeton. That is a story my grandmother would have loved.

In truth, it is a story I love. It is a story about our country's promise: that we are a nation that has decided to come together across historically unknown differences in human history to create a brighter future together. Yes, I could count on my family's support and my own hard work. But I also benefitted from public schools my neighbors paid for, a public safety system and national defense that kept me secure, and a government that employed my father and gave him a decent wage, housing, and health care. No amount of hard work and chutzpah on my end would have amounted to anything without the schooling, safety, food, shelter, and good health I was afforded by our great country.

I love our country. Deeply. Madly. I love the crowded New York restaurants and the backwoods zydeco bars of Louisiana. I love the sound of Chicago's "L" train thundering overhead and the view of a sunset on I-10 in Texas's hill country. I love the smell of the *pupuserias* and Oaxacan restaurants that waft in your car when you drive down Eighth Street in Los Angeles after work on a Tuesday night. I love watching, coffee in hand and sleepy-eyed, the sunrise over Carlin Park in Jupiter, Florida.

I think of this book as a single love letter to my country—one of many I could have written. It is a love letter that proposes that when our daily practice and our national story come together, there is nothing we cannot accomplish.

# RISING INEQUALITY IN AMERICA

# 2

# RISING INCOME INEQUALITY

I can trace the genesis of this book back to a single train ride.

In January 2016, I was commuting home from the Loop to my northside neighborhood on Chicago's "L" train. People packed into the train car. At other times of the year, this can seem unnerving. But on a Chicago January day, the sun sets at four thirty in the afternoon, and early evening temperatures rarely exceed twenty-five degrees. People in puffy coats press close to one another. The darkness outside somehow makes the car more hushed than it would otherwise be. An almost coziness settles in.

I use the twenty-minute ride to unwind.

I try to put distance between me and the workday. Hunched over my phone, I skim the news, on the hunt for interesting stories I may have missed throughout the day. On this January ride, I came across the headline of an Emily Peck article on the *Huffington Post* that grabbed my attention. I thought it was so fantastical it had to be wrong:

"The 62 Richest People on Earth Now Hold as Much Wealth as the Poorest 3.5 Billion."[1]

I clicked on the link. The crux was a newly released Oxfam report that found that sixty-two people indeed had as much wealth as the bottom half of all people in the world.

Not sixty-two families.

Not sixty-two businesses or cities.

Sixty-two people were as wealthy as 3.5 billion people. I reeled. I knew the rich were wealthy, even fabulously wealthy. But I had not imagined that they owned as much as half of the world's population did.

As I wrestled with this, I wondered if I had remained ignorant of this because I am an American. Perhaps, I thought, I was unable to see this appalling wealth concentration because it was due to crushing poverty, corrupt systems, and unjust inequality that existed elsewhere in the world. America was different, I told myself.

Sure, we had wealth. But I believed we had largely eliminated the two-dollar-a-day poverty so prevalent elsewhere in the world. Our country has made great strides—historic strides—to remedy many types of injustice. We have ensured a basic level of health, education, housing, literacy, and political voice for our citizenry that is unparalleled in human history. Former president Barack Obama told the graduating class of Howard University at his commencement address in 2016, "If you had to choose one moment in history in which you could be born and you didn't know ahead of time who you were going to be . . . you'd choose right now."[2]

And I *would* choose right now.

Had I been born fifty years earlier, I would not have risen so far above the economic station of my grandmother.

Had I been born even twenty years earlier, I would not be able to be married to my husband or likely raise my daughter.

I believed America was more fair and more just than almost any other society in human history. This is not to say I was unfamiliar with the tragic burdens of American poverty. I had spent twenty years working in and with low-income communities to make schools better. It is also not to say I was unfamiliar with the heights of American privilege. Having attended elite universities, I had grown close to people with immense wealth. But the inequality we had in America, tragic as it was, was bounded. Or so I thought.

With a mix of curiosity and self-righteousness, I began the hunt for information that would prove me right. I hoped I would find data that would uphold America as a model for the rest of the world. We were not perfect. But we had to be on the front lines of the march to a more equitable global society.

I was wrong.

What I found did not sing the praises of America's relative equality. Instead, I began to learn how the wealth gap in our country is widening at an alarming rate, especially across racial lines. I began to uncover how we are squandering the opportunity to live up to our own values.

—

Mike Espinoza's laugh is both infectious and timid.[3] He is an eager conversationalist. He nods vigorously, then tips forward and rocks back when he is caught up in a point. And when he is delighted, which he often is in conversation, he pulls his head back and snickers quietly.

He is a big man who dresses like a family doctor on summer vacation. Pleated khakis sit high on his waist. He wears knit polo shirts. His phone is always clipped onto a holster at his belt. He has wire-rimmed glasses, and his black hair is thinning to wisps across his head. Today, Mike and his family live in Fresno, California, where his wife is a union leader and he organizes low-income families. But I first met Mike in 2013, halfway across the country. A native of Houston, he worked with me for two years to organize parents and teachers in his hometown. I lived in Los Angeles at the time but flew to Texas regularly to help him do the work.

The thing about Houston is that you spend a lot of time driving around. During these trips, as Mike and I traveled between meetings or to lunch or back to whatever hotel I was staying in, I had the privilege of learning much of his story.

Mike was born on the east side of Houston in 1979 to a Mexican American family that goes back at least six generations in Texas. His parents were devout evangelical Christians. For them, work was almost an afterthought. The church was the real focus of their lives.

"My earliest memories were of children's church," Mike shares, "singing songs and clapping hands." As he grew up, the family oriented their lives around the church's weekly schedule. Monday and Thursday were for Bible study at home; Wednesday was for Bible study at church. Friday was youth service. Saturday was full of church socials. And Sunday was back-to-back church services from early morning through the evenings, with meals interspersed throughout. "Tuesdays were the only days off from church," he remembers.

In the Espinoza family, "work was purely about paying the bills. Work came second to ministry." As a result, they had enough money but never a lot. Mike's dad had worked his way up from the mail room to become a drafter at an engineering firm. But things took a turn when his dad was laid off in the economic downturn of the early 1980s. He had been with the company for years, but one day, it was all over.

The impact shook the Espinoza family. For two years, his dad was out of a job. When Mike was seven years old, the family lost their house. They began living out of their car for several months.

At the end of each school day, Mike's dad would collect him and his siblings from school. They would park at the Burger King at the intersection of Wayside Drive and Harrisburg Boulevard in east Houston. The owner belonged to the same church as Mike's family, and he allowed them to park the car there overnight. Mike's parents sat in the front seat of the station wagon, and his dad would read the Bible until they dozed off. His sister slept in the middle row. And Mike and his brother played around in the back area until they fell asleep. In the morning, they would dig through the trash bags that stored their clothes to pick out their outfits for the day and get dropped off at school.

The free breakfasts and lunches at school were a saving grace. They often stocked up on the food the other kids would leave uneaten. "Pizza day was our favorite," Mike says. "On that day, we would stock up on tater tots."

Eventually, things returned to normal. Mike's dad got a job, and they were able to get their house back. But these memories—and the toll the experience took on his family—burned deep inside of Mike. Almost as deeply as the memory of Pedro's murder.

When Mike turned about twelve or thirteen, he began opting out of the near-daily church activities. As a result, he says, "my brother and I had a lot of alone time. Eventually, he started just running the streets." At first, Mike stayed home. But soon he ventured outside to join his brother and the neighborhood boys. Some of the boys eventually recruited him into low-level schemes: scaring kids who crossed into the neighborhood from nearby Denver Harbor or small-scale theft.

Pedro was one of these boys. He was a little bit older, the first guy in the neighborhood to get a car, and he ran with Mike and his brother. "He had a mouth on him," Mike remembers. "He would talk shit all the time." One day, some guys from a nearby neighborhood came through. There was a sudden and violent altercation. They shot Pedro. "They took his shoes, his Jordans," Mike says. "I remember seeing his white Honda Civic and the windows were bloody and my brother telling me those were his brains. I was sick to my stomach. His mom had the car cleaned and she drove it." Every once in a while, Mike would see Pedro's car roll through the neighborhood. After telling the story, Mike pauses for a long moment before adding, "I'll never forget."

The murder happened in the summer before Mike's ninth grade year. Everything became real in a different way for him. "Suddenly, I knew we had been playing Russian roulette with our lives. It's a miracle. It's a miracle we hadn't been killed. . . . We were playing with fire."

The night of Pedro's funeral, Mike and his brother sat on the street corner under the bright streetlight where everyone would get together and smoke weed. His brother turned to him. "We can't live this way," he said. From then on, Mike started pulling in a totally different direction. He decided not to go to the neighborhood high school. Instead, he joined the ROTC program at a school closer to his grandmother's house.

His senior year, a college recruiter named John Martinez from Franklin & Marshall College in Lancaster, Pennsylvania, began calling "on a daily basis." He was from the same neighborhood and was hell-bent on getting more kids like him to Franklin & Marshall. If he couldn't reach Mike at home, he would call Mike's teachers. Mike was uninterested, even reluctant. But John eventually wore him down. Mike applied, and not only did he get accepted; he earned a scholarship. He didn't know what to do. "I had never been outside of Texas," he explained. "Never really been outside of the neighborhood." His parents were fearful about Mike living so far from home. But Gabe Gabriel, known as "Gabby"—a top dog or, as Mike called him, an "OG" of the neighborhood—pulled him aside. "You got to go," he urged. "There has to be one of us who gets out of this." Mike packed up his car and drove north.

Up until college, Mike didn't have a sense of what forces of poverty held his neighborhood in their grasp. But then his freshman-year roommate talked about his European vacations and bought a new MacBook with his grandfather's credit card. To help make sense of the dichotomies between his childhood scarcity and the lives of his classmates, Mike turned to others who shared his experiences. He got involved in campus Latino politics. He read the writings of Malcolm X, Texas Chicano leader José Angel Gutiérrez, Chicano militant Corky Gonzales, and Cesar Chavez. Mike realized that he had grown up surrounded by poverty.

Many of his white classmates in college had not.

The Chicano activists he read and came to know helped him see how the poverty his neighborhood was steeped in was the direct result of generations of injustice. But it took going away to a largely white school in eastern Pennsylvania for Mike to become radicalized as a Chicano activist.

His understanding further deepened back in Houston when he began working for the Service Employees International Union (SEIU) in 2006 to lead the Justice for Janitors campaign. It was then that he saw how the poverty his community had been forced into stood in stark contrast to the immense wealth of the top income earners in America.

A chasm was widening between the rich, who were getting richer, and Mike's community, which continued to struggle. To see this chasm take shape—to understand Mike's anger as he organized janitors against wealthy business leaders—we have to go back nearly fifty years.

## A Snapshot of Rising Income Inequality

Perhaps the simplest place to begin is by seeing how much more the rich earn today than the average American does. The chasm has not always been this wide.

Let's start by looking at CEO income.

For most of the 1960s and 1970s, CEOs made twenty to thirty times more than the average worker.[4] This twenty-to-one ratio was thought to be the upper limit for how much a CEO could earn while still fostering the sense of teamwork a business needed to thrive. Management guru Peter Drucker was the most ardent advocate for this ratio. Drucker shared that he saw the twenty-to-one salary ratio as "the limit beyond which [managers] cannot go if they don't want resentment and falling morale to hit their companies."[5]

Beginning in the 1980s, however, this wage gap began to expand dramatically. By 1989, CEOs made nearly 60 times the salary of the average worker (Figure 1). By 1995, they took home 122 times more than the average worker. And by 2007, on the eve of the Great Recession, the average CEO earned over 350 times what the average worker did. While the Great Recession brought a bit of a reset, it was not dramatic. In 2011, the average CEO was still making 230 times more than the average worker.[6]

Americans regularly see examples of these widening gaps in our country play out in the news. CEOs issue layoffs to workers even as their own incomes spike. In 2009, one study found that the CEOs who issued the most aggressive layoffs during the recession received 42 percent higher compensation than their peers.[7] In 2014, Pitney Bowes, a company known for its postage meters, laid off nearly 6 percent of its workforce.[8] In that same year, Pitney Bowes more than doubled its CEO's compensation, to nearly $7 million.[9]

Most damning, perhaps, and more recent, is the case of Amazon in 2018. It was a hallmark year for Jeff Bezos, the company's

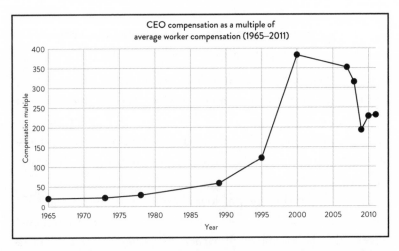

Figure 1. *Source:* Economic Policy Institute, "CEO Compensation and CEO-to-Worker Compensations Ratio, 1965–2011 (2011 Dollars)," The State of Working America, last modified June 18, 2012, http://www.stateofworkingamerica.org/chart/swa-wages-table-4-43-ceo-compensation-ceo/.

founder and CEO. In January, he was named the richest man "ever (or at least in modern times)." His wealth surpassed that of titans like Bill Gates and Warren Buffet.[10] But later in the year, the non-profit New Food Economy released a report on Amazon employees in five states: Arizona, Kansas, Ohio, Washington, and Pennsylvania. Thousands of these workers collected Supplemental Nutrition Assistance Program (SNAP) benefits, popularly known as food stamps, from their state governments. In fact, nearly "one in three Amazon employees in Arizona was on food stamps, or lived with someone who was."[11] Here the richest CEO in modern times was paying his employees such a meager wage that they had to collect food stamps just to feed their families.

But CEOs are not the only people hoarding income.

## Top Income Earners Hoard More of the National Income Than They Have in a Century

A powerful study by economists Thomas Piketty, Emmanuel Saez, and Gabriel Zucman paints an even starker picture. From the end of World War II through 1980, high-income earners and low-income earners in America saw meaningful income growth. Those at the bottom actually saw their wages grow more during this period than top earners.

But as I shared in the previous chapter, beginning in 1980, this changed dramatically. Low-income earners saw their wage growth screech to a halt, while high earners' wages accelerated at break-neck speed. From 1980 to 2014, the median wages for individuals in America increased by 61 percent when controlling for inflation. But by looking only at the average, we obscure a more damning trend. In fact, the top 1 percent of earners saw their wages triple. But the bottom half of earners *saw almost no increase in their wages* (Figure 2).[12]

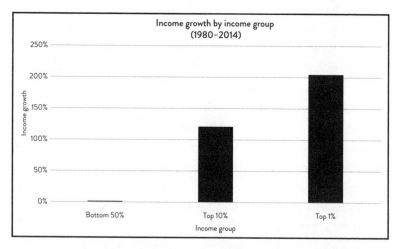

Figure 2. *Source:* Thomas Piketty, Emmanuel Saez, and Gabriel Zucman, *Distributional National Accounts: Methods and Estimates for the United States*, National Bureau of Economic Research (NBER) Working Paper No. 22945, December 2016.

The result?

In 1980, the top 1 percent of earners took home twenty-seven times more each year than the bottom half. By 2014, they were taking home eighty-one times more.[13] Over nearly thirty-five years, the top half of American workers collected all the increase in wages, and the top 1 percent captured most of that.

Two dramatic consequences of this trend emerge. First, we have not seen this level of disparity since the eve of the Great Depression. In 1929, the top 1 percent of earners took home 21 percent of the national income. That didn't happen again until 2006 (Figure 3).

The year 2006 was not an anomaly. It appears to be the new norm. From 2010 to 2014 (the most recent year of data in Piketty's study), the top 1 percent continued to collect nearly a fifth of the nation's income.[14] This income hoarding by the elite stands in stark

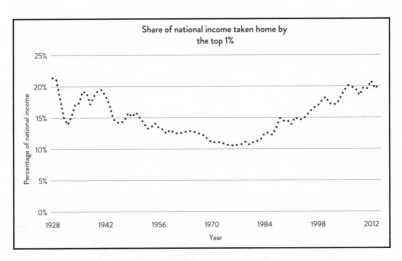

Figure 3. *Source:* Thomas Piketty, Emmanuel Saez, and Gabriel Zucman, *Distributional National Accounts: Methods and Estimates for the United States*, National Bureau of Economic Research (NBER) Working Paper No. 22945, December 2016.

contrast to most of post–World War II America. Between 1960 and 1986, for example, the top 1 percent took home less than 13 percent of the national income annually.[15]

When you layer in how much of the national income the bottom half of earners received, a second disturbing trend emerges. Piketty and his colleagues can measure how much of the national income the members of this group have made from 1962 onward. From 1962 to 1995, the bottom half of earners took home more, collectively, than the top 1 percent. In many years, like the early 1970s, the bottom half took home almost twice as much as the top 1 percent (Figure 4).

But in 1996, the lines crossed. The top 1 percent began bringing in more income than the entire bottom half of American workers. And it gets worse: by 2014, that tiny fraction of people began taking

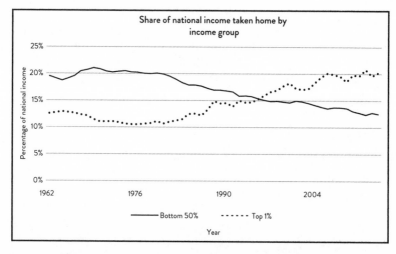

Figure 4. *Source:* Thomas Piketty, Emmanuel Saez, and Gabriel Zucman, *Distributional National Accounts: Methods and Estimates for the United States,* National Bureau of Economic Research (NBER) Working Paper No. 22945, December 2016.

home nearly *twice* as much as the bottom half of all workers each year. And the gap shows no signs of slowing.

In case some may speculate that this widening gap is merely a function of modern capitalism, I want to point out that this gap between top and bottom earners in America is not seen by our peers in western Europe. In 1980, the picture in the United States and western Europe looked largely the same. The bottom half of earners took home roughly twice as much as the top 1 percent. But while these lines crossed in the United States in 1996, in Europe, they remained largely fixed. By 2016, the bottom half of earners in Europe were still taking home nearly twice as much of the national income as the top 1 percent.[16] America is rare among peer countries in our willingness to allow our top earners to outearn median workers by so much.

When you pan out to examine family income in America and not just individual income, you see that top households are getting richer faster. Let's look back to the postwar boom: From the end of World War II until 1979, families at all levels saw their incomes rise. In fact, once again, the households at the bottom enjoyed a greater rise in income than top-earning families did.

In 1979, a gap emerged. Between 1979 and 2007, the wages of bottom-earning families stagnated, while higher-earning households enjoyed an increase (Figure 5). The richer you were, the faster your household's income rose.[17]

But this is not just a story of who is capturing economic growth. It is also about who is insulated when the economy takes a downturn. With the onset of the Great Recession, the bottom 95 percent of households all saw their incomes drop, with low-income families enduring the steepest decline. But the top 5 percent of families actually experienced wage growth (Figure 6).

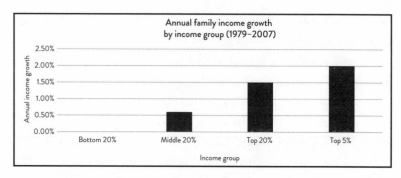

Figure 5. *Source:* Economic Policy Institute, "Average Family Income Growth, by Income Group, 1947–2013," The State of Working America, last modified September 25, 2014, http://stateofworkingamerica.org/chart/swa-income -figure-2m-change-real-annual/.

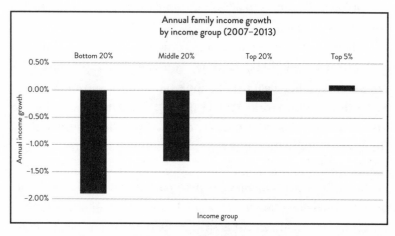

Figure 6. *Source:* Economic Policy Institute, "Average Family Income Growth, by Income Group, 1947–2013," The State of Working America, last modified September 25, 2014, http://stateofworkingamerica.org/chart/swa-income -figure-2m-change-real-annual/.

Put together, we see that between 1979 and 2010, the median family income grew by 14 percent overall. But the family income for the top 1 percent grew ten times faster.[18]

## Justice for Janitors

These inequalities don't merely exist in policy papers and graphs. Everyday Americans are reeling from the impact of this rising income gap.

Mike had been back in Houston for nearly four years before he came on board with SEIU in its campaign to better the working conditions of the city's janitors. He had worked as a high school teacher, printed a radical Chicano paper out of his parents' basement, and earned his master's degree at the Center for Mexican American Studies at the University of Houston. But it was his efforts as the primary coordinator of the massive Houston May Day rallies in 2006, opposing the draconian immigration bills being pushed through Congress at the time, that caught SEIU's eye. With his support, the May Day rally became the largest protest ever held before in Houston.

His friends at SEIU were impressed. At that point, many private sector janitors in Houston were hired by a small number of janitorial firms and farmed out to most of the office buildings in the city. These janitors were being paid minimum wage—$5.15 an hour—and most only worked four hours a day. SEIU was working to get these firms to recognize the union as the collective bargaining unit for these janitors and to increase their wages by 50 cents an hour. The slogan for SEIU's campaign was "There's no future on $20 a day."

Coming off the most active phase of the immigration protests, Mike was eager for more. He joined eleven other activists in November 2006 as they chained themselves to trash cans in the middle of one of the busiest intersections in downtown Houston. They sought to bring awareness to their organizing campaign for local janitors. The action worked, garnering a ton of press and mobilizing hundreds of people. Mike was hooked.

In 2007, he began his work by meeting with the janitors, building relationships and earning their trust. He listened to their stories. Many were here as immigrants.

"I came here escaping domestic violence in Mexico," they shared.

"I came here for a better life."

"We had to dodge Border Patrol on the crossing."

"I lost my brother on the way over here."

Once they found their way to Houston, their cousin or a friend of a friend hooked them up with a job. But they didn't have a markedly better life. They cleaned in the office buildings in the anonymity of night, earning twenty dollars a shift. They could barely make ends meet.

"Our lights just got turned off," one told Mike.

"I work multiple jobs."

"I work seven days a week."

Then Mike and the SEIU team would go meet with the management. "I remember one manager had a gold ring on almost every finger," Mike shared. "And the bosses above him were all white, all corporate types. They were all about the business plan, the business model, the business implications." They weren't about the stories or the people.

The initial campaign saw some big wins. An agreement with the biggest cleaning companies in 2006 earned the janitors a pay raise to $7.75 an hour over two years. Then the 2008 financial crisis hit. Big banks and major corporations took government bailout money. By 2012, an economic upswing was underway. Janitors began pushing for an increase to $10 an hour. But even as the economy bounced back, the cleaning companies and their clients exhibited little willingness to pay the janitors a living wage. Mike was no longer working with SEIU at that time, but he was still part of the broader organizing community in Houston. In 2012, SEIU shared that Fortune 500 companies saw a 30 percent increase in profits over the previous year. These companies' CEOs saw their pay increase 50 percent in the same period. But one in five people in Houston that year still earned less than $10 an hour.[19]

Mike's ire is particularly focused on Jamie Dimon, the famed CEO of JPMorgan Chase. The bank was the major tenant of one of the largest buildings in downtown Houston, a building with a janitors' union. Dimon's bank took a $12 billion bailout in 2008 but said it couldn't afford to ensure the janitors who cleaned its offices in Houston had a living wage. In 2012, Jamie Dimon earned nearly $42 million in compensation. SEIU ran some numbers and estimated it would take a Houston janitor 2,500 years to earn what Dimon earned in that one year.

Shareholders are earning massive returns, and executives rake in huge salaries. But the local cleaning companies bemoan paying their janitors $10 an hour. After his childhood experiences, college consciousness-raising, and involvement in organizing for immigrant rights, Mike thought he understood the contours of inequality. But it took the Justice for Janitors campaigns to open his eyes to it on this level.

"My view of wealth when I was coming up and as an activist was someone who had a two-story home and a nice car," Mike remembers. But to learn of the massive wealth businesses were returning to shareholders and their executives, juxtaposed against the stories of struggle and penury his janitors dealt with, was inequality at a wholly different scale.

## Not All Income Earners Bear This Injustice Equally

Our discussion up to now has focused on our society at large, which can obfuscate some alarming realities. When we disaggregate income inequality by race and gender, we see trends that reinforce troubling systemic divides in our country.

For example, when we separate the data by race, we see that white families in America take home 57 percent more in household income than Black families and 37 percent more than Latino families.[20] This gap has proven to be remarkably steady over the past forty-five years.[21] Systemic racism in all its forms upholds this inequality.

When we focus on gender, we see a similarly unequal picture. In 2017, the median woman worker in America took home 80 percent of what the median man took home.[22] There are many reasons. Certainly how we value home care as well as childbirth and child-rearing plays a role. Systemic gender discrimination in the workplace also contributes to this inequality. The widespread public narrative over #MeToo only begins to shine a light on the ways in which rampant sexual harassment, merely one form of gender discrimination, often blocks women from assuming high-paying roles for which they are qualified.

As you can imagine, when you layer race and gender on top of each other, the resulting picture is even more damning. Latinas only earn 54 percent of what white men earn. Black women earn less than two-thirds.[23]

While most of this project will explore the ways inequality writ large is growing in America, it is important to acknowledge that it is disproportionately borne by women and people of color. My proposal for change must be paired with other thoughtful proposals to tackle systemic racial and gender discrimination if we are going to address economic inequality meaningfully and holistically in our country.

—

Today, Mike Espinoza lives in Fresno, California, with his wife and two stepchildren. He has the two-story house he thought signified wealth when he was a kid. He confesses that they even have a small pool (a near necessity in a town where average temperatures approach 100 degrees in July). He is a far cry from living out of his family's station wagon or running the streets with Pedro. But even though Mike's economic situation has improved dramatically, he is many degrees of magnitude further removed from the top 1 percent of earners, who are making out like bandits.

We saw how from the 1950s through much of the 1970s, the incomes of the highest earners were tied much more closely to the incomes of the median workers. At that time, the bottom half of all earners in America took home more income than the top 1 percent. But beginning in the 1980s, the incomes of the top earners began to skyrocket well above the average worker. No longer are the janitors, the middle-class organizers like Mike and his wife, and the CEOs improving their respective lots together. Income inequality unlike anything we have seen in a century began to settle in.

Annual incomes are only part of the story though.

# 3

# RISING WEALTH INEQUALITY

Joanna Williams and I ate sushi at Sugarfish on Seventh Street in downtown Los Angeles. The room glowed, softly backlit by indigo and crimson neon.[1] It set the scene for a casual conversation. Joanna's black wavy hair frames a face dominated by expressive eyes and a wide dynamic smile. She had been assigned a few weeks prior to work with me and my team on enhancing our diversity and equity practices. This was her first trip to LA and our first time spending meaningful time together in person.

From the moment we connected on the phone, I could feel that Joanna was a maelstrom in the best of ways. She is a quiet listener and a dynamic speaker. She embodies both intensity and light-heartedness as a social justice practitioner who is trained in comedy improv. She brings together powerful and often opposing currents in a single churning mix. And she named something in me that night over sushi I had never been able to put a finger on before.

Ever since I was a kid, I told her, I had felt I existed with a foot in two worlds, never fully belonging to either. I am a gay Christian—a progressive who grew up in a conservative family. And our family relocated so much that after each move, I felt similarly like I belonged to neither my previous town nor the new one. I don't know what prompted me to share all of this, but I confessed I didn't have a way of explaining or even understanding what this meant for me.

She looked at me and succinctly and rapidly responded, "Oh yeah, it's what I call in-betweenness. It's how I grew up too."

Joanna was born in a white working-class neighborhood in a rust belt American city. Her father grew up in an orphanage not far from Dhaka, the capital of Bangladesh. He lived in such poverty that he survived on one meal a day. But some priests saw something special in him and helped him get a scholarship to a local high school. Joanna's father did so well that he went to college, and eventually, the same priests awarded him a scholarship to study psychology on a six-month visa. "Four months in, he didn't want to leave. So he stayed in America. He didn't return home for another thirty years."

Joanna's mom was born to solid blue-collar European stock in middle America. The family didn't have a ton of resources, so she often helped out with childcare for her younger siblings. When she was old enough to leave home, she too benefitted from the church. She took a job as an administrator in a downtown Catholic cathedral.

By the time Joanna's parents met, married, and had her, they were struggling financially. Joanna's dad was studying to become a psychologist and working nights. Her mom was employed during the day as a secretary. "They were just miserable," Joanna remembers. But then they came into a bit of family money, her dad started working in financial services, and they were able to buy a small home. Things got easier at that point.

The result of these shifts in her parents' lives—from being beneficiaries of the Catholic Church, to scraping to get by, to a solid middle-class life—was that Joanna inherited two conflicting value systems. "One was you need to sacrifice for the world's good. The other was you need to make a shit ton of money." Joanna was caught between these polar pulls.

As a half Asian and half European child growing up in the Midwest, she felt neither fully white nor welcomed as fully Asian. During her time in high school, she became friends with a diverse group of Asian American girls. At one point in her junior year, she remembers saying, "Isn't it cool we're all friends? We're all Asian." One girl looked at her and replied, "You're not Asian." Joanna got really angry. "Who are these people?" she remembers thinking. "My dad was born in Asia. Why do I need to go prove that I'm Asian?" But she felt in-between nonetheless.

By the time she attended a small liberal arts college on the East Coast, the tensions embedded in her life—being Asian and white, feeling pressure to make money but also serve the world—led her to bounce around. She interned at a legal defense fund in France, worked at a major law firm, volunteered at a halfway house in Mexico, applied to do strategy consulting for major American corporations, and prepared to enroll in a PhD program. The work of being in-between was taking its toll. She was living with friends in DC, working part-time jobs, and feeling rudderless.

Fortunately, a friend at her church put her in touch with a community organizer who in turn introduced her to a woman who ran an immigrant rights group. She started as an intern, working twelve hours a week on social media outreach for the burgeoning national campaign for immigration reform. Soon, she realized this was the work she was meant to be doing. At this job, she could be one part theorist and one part practitioner. She could handle the logistical work of putting on major events and simultaneously build relationships with stakeholders. She was able to hold her many identities together. She decided against pursuing her PhD, and by January of 2007, she was working full-time organizing around immigration reform.

Joanna's in-betweenness set her up to see things around her that others missed. You know that joke about the two fish? One fish says to the other, "Good morning. How's the water?" The second fish replies, "What's water?" When you have been immersed in something—a community, an ideology, a set of experiences—it is hard to see it for what it is. Joanna's in-betweenness allowed her to see things that others who were firmly situated in only one experience could not. And what Joanna is particularly good at seeing is power. She sees how power forms, how it excludes, and who it benefits.

As she launched her job as an organizer, she witnessed and built relationships with people experiencing the injustices of the American economic and political systems. Prior to organizing, she "had all the words of academia" to make sense of the inequities around her, but the academic worldview didn't fully jibe with her own personal experiences, and it didn't talk enough about power. But in organizing, a deep understanding of power was central to the work. In the immigration space at this time, there was a "huge ramp-up of ICE raids. This was the first wave of public exposure about women chained while they're trying to give birth. The first round of people seeing kids being separated from their families." To fight these injustices, the immigration reform campaign had to isolate who had the power to make a change and identify what those people cared about. They then would use that understanding to push those leaders to make a change.

In 2009, Joanna left the immigrants' rights work and moved to a small, predominantly white town of thirty thousand people a few hours north of New York City to deepen her relationship with her now-husband. Today, she is the CEO of a local consulting group that works with individuals and teams to drive high-impact change projects. In this work, she is able to use many of her identities—as an academic, an organizer, a planner, a woman of color, even an improv actor—to get at real change at a local level.

When I bring up the subject of rising wealth inequality in the US, she meets it with nods of recognition. She has seen this trend play out in her work across the country. She has seen it play out in her adopted hometown. And her in-betweenness—her ability to straddle so many worlds authentically—gives her unique insight into understanding it. She encourages me to think about power.

—

The story of income is like a picture. It describes what one earner or household takes home in a defined period of time. But the story of wealth is like a movie, depicting how wages and property and market returns pool over time and across generations.

We should rightly be alarmed by the rising inequality we see in wages. We should be downright frightened by the rising inequality we see in wealth.

What do I mean by wealth? In short, wealth is everything we own minus everything we owe. It is our homes, our cars, our bank accounts, and our retirement accounts. Add that all up and subtract our student loans, mortgage balances, and credit card debt and you get someone's wealth, sometimes called their net worth. The thing about wealth is that it is cumulative. It starts with everything given to us by our families. To that, we add all the wealth we accumulate. If our families are wealthy (they own a lot and they owe little in comparison), we have a higher mountain of wealth to build upon. If our families lack wealth, we start from ground zero—or some-times even below that.

As we will see, wealth begets wealth. But it's about more than inheritance. It's about accessing all the networks and opportunities that make building wealth more likely. This is part of what Joanna encourages me to explore. If your family has enough wealth and enough connections ("power") to send you to the best schools, ensure you are healthy enough to focus on your education, get you out of minor trouble at school or with the law, introduce you to potential employers who might give you your first job, and help you start your career off with no debt, you are incredibly well set up to add to your wealth. In this way, the rich have been growing their wealth and power across generations at a remarkable pace over the past fifty years.

In the 1960s, as we have seen, America's economy was charging forward. During this time of strong economic growth, the top 1 percent of households and the bottom 90 percent of households held equal amounts of wealth.[2] For the next twenty years, we saw little change in this. Household wealth grew during this time. And it grew by similar amounts for households at all wealth bands.

But at some point in the 1980s, similar to what we saw with income, we began to see a growing divergence in household wealth. From 1983 through the eve of the Great Recession, the wealth for the top 20 percent grew nearly twice as fast as it did for the rest of America.[3] Through the years immediately following the Great Recession, this wealth gap widened even more quickly.[4] The result is staggering. By 2010, the average household in the top 1 percent owned 288 times the wealth of the median US household (Figure 7).[5]

Let's look at this another way: by 2016, the top 1 percent no longer owned as much as the bottom 90 percent; they owned twice as much.[6]

I want to scream this to every person in America.

Take the wealth of almost every household in our country—the bottom 90 percent.

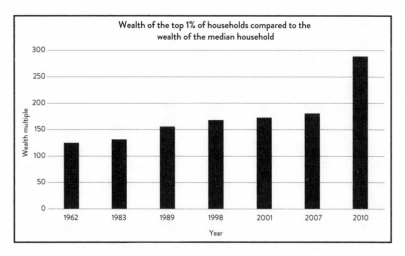

Figure 7. *Source:* Economic Policy Institute, "Change in Average Real Annual Household Income, by Income Group, 1979–2010," The State of Working America, last modified August 10, 2012, http://stateofworkingamerica.org/chart/swa-income-figure-2m-change-real-annual/.

These are our factory workers and farmers.

Our restaurant workers and plumbers.

Our accountants and teachers.

These are even many of our doctors and lawyers and university professors.

Take everything they own—all their wealth—and put it in one giant pile. That pile only equals *half* of what the top 1 percent own.

A *Washington Post* headline in December 2017 shared, "The richest 1 percent now owns more of the country's wealth than at any time in the past 50 years."[7] To put it in even more frightening terms: by 2013, the wealthiest families in America owned nearly as much of our national wealth as they did on the eve of the Great Depression.[8] *We are at Roaring Twenties, pre-stock-market-crashing inequality right now.* That should cause all of us great alarm.

For Joanna, there is no way to understand this rising wealth inequality without talking about power. On one level, it is about who benefits from the current system and how they are using the power the system gives them to reinforce those benefits. As corporations have acquired more political power, shareholders and senior executives have used it to bend the economy to reinforce their positions. This is what Joanna calls "the psychotic restructuring of what is good in America." The more economic and political power top earners and owners accrue, the more they hoard. That is how we've come to see the top 1 percent own twice as much as the bottom 90 percent. It is not through one decision here or a single policy there. It is through a systematic effort to allow the rich to hoard wealth. We have enabled this by lowering corporate tax rates. Taxing stock market profits less than we tax income earned from labor. Instilling favorable inheritance structures. Funding schools mostly through local property taxes, which means rich neighborhoods give more to schools than poor neighborhoods do. And so on and so on and so on.

———

There is a deeper dynamic here. And there is no way to really talk about power in the American economy without discussing the traumas of racism and misogyny.

Joanna sits against a bare living room wall. The top of her couch peeks over the bottom border of my iPad screen. I am calling from my screened-in porch on a type of midwestern day where the promise of spring outpaces its actual warmth. The sky is blue and green leaves are finally budding on trees, but I am dressed in a long-sleeved knit shirt. By the looks of Joanna's light short-sleeved shirt, spring is being far more generous in the Northeast.

I knew that community organizing, particularly around immigrant rights, was a calling for Joanna. It allowed her to build relationships and coordinate campaigns, all for a cause she was deeply committed to. And she was good at it. So I didn't really understand yet why she left.

Even in the immigrant rights organizing space, she shared, the understanding of power didn't fully mesh with her experiences. The power analysis she and her colleagues were using was too narrow and too focused on achieving the immediate win in front of them. It didn't seek to uncover and dismantle the broader systems. "We talked about power in the way of, 'How do you get people to do something?' We didn't talk about power [to help] people deeply understand white supremacy culture." Joanna pushed me to see how the power structures that uphold racism and misogyny and capitalism are deeply intertwined.

Similar to the income gap, the wealth gap does not affect all groups equally. It harms those from historically marginalized communities even more dramatically. This is particularly true when we look at how the wealth gap plays out by race.

The year 1963 was not a particularly equitable time in American racial history. The Civil Rights Act and Voting Rights Act had not yet been passed. Medgar Evers, the first Black field secretary of the NAACP in Mississippi, was assassinated. At this time, the average wealth for white families was slightly more than seven times greater than the wealth of nonwhite families.

However, despite the successes of the civil rights movement, wealth inequality between white and nonwhite families has barely improved since then. By 2010, the average wealth for white families was still nearly seven times that of Black families and nearly five times that of Latino families.[9] Today, only seven of the wealthiest four hundred Americans (1.75 percent) are Black or Latino.[10]

When we look at how wealth gets passed down from generation to generation, we see how the intersections of poverty and race continue to fuel each other. In 1989, the most recent year of data of this kind, 24 percent of white households inherited wealth from a previous generation. Their average inheritance was $145,000. For Black households, the numbers were a fraction of this: only 6 percent of Black households inherited wealth. Their average inheritance was also less than a third of what whites received: $42,000.[11]

A cursory review of underlying data suggests this is not improving any time soon. Two major factors for accruing wealth in modern America—homeownership and education—disproportionately favor white households over households of color. Let's start with housing. Nearly three-fourths (73 percent) of white households own their own homes, while fewer than half of Latino families (47 percent) and Black families (45 percent) do.[12] Richard Rothstein points out in his remarkably researched *The Color of Law* how this massive gap in homeownership is not accidental. In fact, it is the result of decades of intentional government action.[13] Racial zoning limited where Black families could rent or buy homes. The state enforced restrictive covenants barring the sale of property to Black owners. In the most egregious cases, police used violence to intimidate Black families from moving into predominantly white neighborhoods.

Perhaps most wide-reaching was the exclusion of most Black families from Federal Housing Authority (FHA)–backed loans. Launched by the National Housing Act of 1934, the FHA sought to boost home construction and ownership by insuring mortgage lenders from a loss if a qualified borrower defaulted. This meant that banks were more willing to extend mortgages to homeowners, knowing that the federal government would help the bank limit its losses if homeowners defaulted. As a result, more people secured mortgages and bought homes. Soon, however, the FHA refused to back loans in primarily Black communities. It deemed these loans an imprudent extension of credit. The FHA drew maps to assign risk to various neighborhoods, and communities in which they would not back mortgages were colored red. As a result, the practice of refusing to back mortgages in Black neighborhoods was called "redlining."

The FHA program has been called by some the single largest transfer of wealth in American history. But it largely excluded Black families. Through zoning restrictions, real estate practices, intimidation, and violence, Black families throughout America were largely limited to living in predominantly Black neighborhoods—the same areas for which the FHA would not guarantee loans. Banks therefore would not extend mortgages to Black families in these neighborhoods. The result is that the massive boon the FHA provided white families to accumulate wealth in their homes largely passed Black families by. A generation of white families acquired real estate wealth while Black families were left with little.

The rental market was also affected by all this state action. As Black families were stymied from owning homes, they were simultaneously forced to pay higher rates for the homes they were permitted to rent. As far back as the 1920s, a city of Chicago study found that Black residents were paying 20 percent more for housing than white families for similar homes.[14] A simple law of supply and demand played out. Since Black people were permitted to live in only a few neighborhoods, landlords could therefore charge higher rents for the properties in these neighborhoods. Black families, who had few places to move to, had little option but to accept these higher rates. At the same time, Black workers were paid less than white workers for their labor and often excluded from labor unions and the benefits they provided. As Black families plowed more of their already reduced income into higher rents, they could divert less into savings or other wealth accumulation.

As these policies came together, our government subsidized and supported white families in growing their wealth through residential real estate while blocking Black families from doing the same. Played out across generations, this racial wealth gap grew even wider.

The schoolhouse is another place we have used to promote the racial wealth gap. Education is key to a person's ability to increase their eventual wages and therefore wealth. Yet educational opportunities are not equally afforded to young people of color. One-third of all school funding in America comes from local property taxes.[15] This means that wealthy communities like Beverly Hills are going to be able to invest much more in their schools than communities like Compton can invest in theirs, even though these two cities are only twenty-five miles apart. In a country with massive racial segregation, the result is that in America we spend over $2,000 more for every student who attends a predominantly white school than we do for every student who attends a predominantly nonwhite school.[16]

As a result of a host of inequities, not simply school funding, 86 percent of white students graduate from high school, while only 73 percent of Latino students and 69 percent of Black students do.[17] When we look further down the road to college graduation, a gap persists and even widens. In 2015, 21 percent of young Black people had college degrees, but among young white people, 43 percent did.[18] In other words, white young people were twice as likely to graduate from college as their Black peers.

Just as we saw how the racial income gap predicted the racial wealth gap, there may be a strong link between the gender income gap and a gender wealth gap. However, this is harder to uncover. One possible reason is that we often measure wealth by household, and genders often comingle to create households. However, we do have some data that helps illuminate a troubling wealth gap. One study pointed out that women are 80 percent more likely to live

in poverty in retirement, which reflects in large part the difference in accumulated wealth over working-age years between men
and women.[19] Another study suggests that white women own just
32 percent of what white men own. For women of color, this picture
is even starker. The median net worth for Black women was $200
and for Latinas was $100.[20]

In the end, Joanna presses, we have to acknowledge that we have
an economy that permits the exploitation of certain people over
others. And that exploitation is particularly rampant for women
and people of color. Our economy is premised on "morally bankrupt ethics."

"But how do you get to morally bankrupt ethics?" she asks. "We
didn't just say 'We want to be shits.'" We got here, she believes,
"because we have generations of unresolved trauma, which makes
more and more people complicit in the fucked-up moral economy
[we] are talking about." Four hundred years ago, when we decided
to build the American economy on the enslavement of Black people
and the genocide and forced resettlement of Native Americans,
we were sowing seeds of exploitation that live on today. For centuries, we have upheld that women's labor is not worth the same as
men's, so it should be unsurprising that women today accrue less
wealth than their male counterparts.

To undo these harms will take generations of sacrifice and hon-
esty and commitment to one another. No one solution will absolve
us of these national sins. But broadening our definition of the owners and intended beneficiaries of economic success to include all of
us equally has to be part of the solution. Expanding who has power
and who benefits from that power is essential.

In order to expand that circle of benefits and ownership, we
have to acknowledge how the alarming picture of wage inequality
we saw earlier has compounded over decades to create a damning

exposé of wealth inequality and how both sets of inequality come together to disadvantage people of color and women at even greater levels. We are racing forward at breakneck speed to create levels of disparity that far exceed the irresponsible and un-American ones that precipitated the Great Depression. In order to slow down—or better, reverse course—we have to understand what has brought us here. As the wage gap increases, and as homeownership and educational attainment continue to privilege people who already benefit from systemic advantages, we have to ask ourselves, How did we get here? And even more importantly, What is the end game?

# 4

# WHY ECONOMIC INEQUALITY IS RISING

The Chicago winter wind whips down Wabash Avenue like a herd of stockyard cattle corralled by the high canyon walls of skyscrapers. Behind me, perched on corroding umber pillars in the middle of the street, the "L" platform looms two stories up. When the train rumbles cautiously through, the din echoing off the buildings forces conversations around me to stop. To my left, an old English pub advertises Chicago-style pizza and Bud Light in bright neon signage. To my right is the ramp for a parking garage. Ahead of me a narrow building, maybe only twenty feet wide, squeezes in, with no space between it and the buildings to either side, its ornamental facade dirtied and smoothed out by decades of harsh winters and exhaust.

I pull on the door, jerking it open a bit to force the pressure differential to give. Warm lobby air rushes out and I scurry inside to leave the wet wind behind me. I ride up a few flights in a three-person elevator and walk into an inviting greeting area where a soft gray carpet fills the floor. The warm ceiling light is a welcome change from the dull gray outside. I am not sure if this is what I imagined the entrance to a major American labor union might look like, but this is the foyer of UNITE HERE—the hotel workers' union. I tell the receptionist I am here to see the union's national immigration director, Father Clete Kiley.

Soon, Father Clete opens the locked door to the right of the reception desk. Seventy years old, with hair that is still salt-and-pepper (although far more salt than pepper), he has the warm and easy smile of a young man. Making kind small talk, Father Clete escorts me through a warren of cubicles to his cramped office, where we sit down at a small table in the corner. Surrounding him, on shelves and walls and his desktop, are pictures of him with luminaries—celebrities of the global Catholic Church, of Chicago, of the labor movement.

The conversation we share is easy. He is quick to find humor and express delight, filling our time with stories of Chicago and its quirky leaders. We skim the surface of deep waters that have fueled our respective work in justice. Father Clete is clearly someone who knows a good deal about our city. He holds great wisdom and insight into its people, from custodian to cardinal.

I leave that day knowing I want to learn from him and arrange to meet once again. If I am going to understand how these chasms of inequality have set in over the past few decades, I could use the insight of someone who has witnessed them take shape. And a pinch of social justice and a dash of church won't hurt.

———

It's hard to be more Chicago than Clete Kiley.[1] His South Side roots run long and deep. Hearing him speak of his forebearers, some dating back a few centuries, it is easy to get lost in the mix of Irish immigrants and German farmers. But the whole primordial stew of his lineage had settled in Chicago by the late nineteenth century. His great-great-grandfather Patrick Nolan was a trustee of the town of Lake prior to it being annexed by the city of Chicago in 1889 and eventually becoming the neighborhood of Englewood.

Clete grew up at Eighty-Second and Washtenaw in Ashburn, a neighborhood in the heart of blue-collar Irish Chicago. Even as the makeup of the South Side Chicago neighborhoods changed over the decades, Ashburn remained predominantly Irish and Catholic up until the 1990s.

The second oldest of six children, Clete was born in a community just coming out of decades of shared sacrifice and suffering. His parents and grandparents raised him with stories of hardships recently survived. Like the neighbor family with ten kids who ate onion sandwiches to get by. Or the families with fathers who couldn't earn enough to provide for them. Or the sons of both rich and poor families who went off to war and never came back.

What was left from the crater of these tragedies was a commitment to take care of one another. As a young girl, Clete's mother, Rosemary, shepherded extra food her own mother would bake to families struggling to get by. Clete's grandfather, Rosemary's father, started out with just two years of high school education and worked his way up to become an accountant and then a vice president for General Motors. He was able to pull his own family through the Depression and the war, but still he felt he owed something to those around him.

"My parents and their friends had to pull together to get out of the Depression," Clete shared. "Everybody was in it together when we defeated Hitler. We had to be together. There had to be a place for everyone." And in this community where people came together, there was reverence for Roosevelt and the Catholic Church. "You could have put Jesus, Mary, Joseph, and Franklin Roosevelt on the same wall."

The church was the great equalizer. Everyone showed up, and they sat together. Even the most powerful sat in the pews and often served in church volunteer roles. The head usher was a state senator. "In one setting, they were the big guys, right? But in another setting, it's like here, you're no better than me. Matter of fact, you're passing the basket and I'm putting money in it."

As Clete grew up, the Cold War set in and another narrative began to take shape in his neighborhood. A deep pride in America grew and a contrasting narrative began to harden. Not only were we an "incredible country," but we were "the luckiest people in the world . . . [especially] in contrast with all the poor people under the Soviet Bloc." There were enough Eastern European immigrants in the neighborhood to underscore that difference. "You would hear stories of how people's families got out of Hungary or Lithuania and how bad it really was."

His neighbors emphasized "how lucky we were that everybody had a chance, that if you were willing to work hard, you could do well here. It didn't mean you'd become a Rockefeller, but it meant you would have a good life and provide for your family."

At the same time, his neighborhood's and city's deep divisions were bubbling up. Certainly, the Irish Catholic pride of the 1950s and 1960s was on full display. In 1955, "one of [their] own"— Irish Catholic Richard J. Daley—was elected mayor of Chicago. In 1960, another Irish Catholic earned the presidency. But deep racial tension was seething around him. When Chicago South Sider Emmett Till, only seven years older than Clete, was killed on a trip to Mississippi in 1955, many white South Side Chicagoans believed that the horrific murder was the result of the foreign sin of southern bigotry. But as their own neighborhoods began to racially change, Chicago's native local bigotry came out in public like rarely before. Clete remembers the sense of panic among white families in neighborhoods around Ashburn. In 1960, the South Shore neighborhood in Chicago was 90 percent white. By 1970, it had transitioned to 70 percent Black. No one wanted to be the last white family on the block, so people fled. "People sold their houses and would move out at midnight with no forwarding address," he said. They knew their neighbors would feel betrayed.

In 1966, Dr. Martin Luther King Jr. came to Chicago to help catalyze the Chicago Freedom Movement. His time in the city would give rise to his claim that Chicago was one of the most racist cities in America. Clete remembers the day King led an open housing march. Fathers on his block told their kids to "get a rock and go up there to see if you can hit him [King]." The march that day was brutal. Seven hundred white protestors surrounded King "hurling bricks, bottles, and rocks."[2] King was hit in the head by one of those rocks and crumpled to one knee before being ushered onward by his supporters. The following Sunday, Clete sat in the pews and listened as the parish priest chastised his parishioners who had gone to the march to incite violence. "You're Roman Catholics and you're up there throwing rocks at a minister?!" the priest scolded. "What's the matter with you?"

Impassioned with a sense of justice and enamored of the bravery of this priest, Clete thought he might want to become a priest someday. Six years later, he accepted his first assignment at a church in the predominantly Mexican neighborhood of Little Village. For the next three decades, he bounced between local neighborhood ministry (in mostly Latino communities) and church leadership. He studied liberation theology with philosopher and theologian Rev. Gustavo Gutiérrez and served as a leader in the archdiocesan seminary. He worked as a parish priest and as a member of Cardinal Joseph Bernardin's cabinet.

"Father Clete, you are one part radical and one part company man," I pointed out.

"I know," he laughed.

As he rose in influence in the church, he witnessed how the gap between the wealthy and everyone else he served seemed to widen. Immigrants from Latin America were coming to Chicago because they saw America as the "shining city on the hill." But these immigrants, Clete's adopted community, were being lied to and used by the powerful. The economic leaders of the day said we were a country that welcomed immigrants but these leaders "wanted them cheap . . . [with] no benefits and no political power." Clete watched how in his city and across the country the "holders of wealth [are] a smaller and smaller and smaller group of people." And these holders of wealth did not treat workers or immigrants with a sense of shared dignity.

In the mid-1990s, the Director of Ecumenism and Human Relations for the archdiocese, the revered Monsignor Jack Egan, asked Clete to meet with leadership from the Hotel Employees and Restaurant Employees (HERE) union. HERE had launched a campaign to organize frontline workers at O'Hare Airport and wanted Catholic leadership to support them. Clete got involved and his relationship with labor took off.

The stories of workers being fired for speaking their native language at work angered Clete, as did the power imbalances he saw at jobsites. Management's efforts to quash the union appalled him. So much of what he saw spit in the tradition of his church. "God was the first worker," Clete reminded me. For Clete, work derives its inherent dignity directly from God. Therefore, when workers' humanity and dignity are denied, it is not just a political affront but also a theological one.

By 2010, Clete's commitment to the labor cause was fully formed. Coming on the heels of the 2008 economic collapse, he saw how the most vulnerable among us, the poor and the immigrant, were the most harmed. In fact, those most at fault for causing the crisis seemed to skate by almost unscathed. The trend of the economically powerful taking advantage of the most vulnerable was only getting worse. He took on the role of Director of Immigration Policy at UNITE HERE—the national hotel and restaurant workers' union, which is one of the most powerful unions in America. It was in this role that he was able to intertwine his career-long commitments to both immigrants and workers.

———

Clete's story reflects many of the seismic shifts taking place in our country. His journey from growing up as an Irish Catholic boy on Chicago's South Side to becoming an immigrant rights leader in the national labor movement mirrors the dramatic changes our country underwent in the same period.

History often presents a narrative of inevitability. In hindsight, the study of how events unfold takes on a veneer of cosmic inertia. It appears the forces at play had no choice but to flow forth the way they did.

I think the study of the rise of inequality in America may at first suggest that such inequality was inevitable, that there was no other way for events to have unfolded. Inequality may look like the natural by-product of our vibrant economy of growth, innovation, and entrepreneurialism.

But real factors have produced these levels of inequality; they are extensions of decisions we have collectively made about how to structure our economy and our society. Recognizing some of them, and seeing them as social choices, is essential to understanding how we have arrived here. While it would be beyond the scope of this book to lay out all the causes that have fueled our rising inequality, a cursory review of six of them is helpful in creating the political appetite to make different societal choices. Here I borrow from Nobel Prize–winning economist Angus Deaton and others, whose framework explains in some part how our current levels of inequality began to take shape in the 1970s and 1980s.

## Globalization and Immigration

By almost any measure, globalization has skyrocketed over the past few decades. Financial markets are more transnational. The flow of stocks and bonds across borders has increased fifty-four-fold between 1970 and the late 2000s.[3] The decrease of telephone costs and the introduction of the internet have rapidly accelerated transnational communications. Sales by US companies' affiliates in other countries have grown from almost $3 trillion in 1982 to over $31 trillion in 2007.[4] Even the number of international tourists tripled between 1980 and 2009.[5] No matter how you slice it, more people are communicating, traveling, and conducting business on an international scale.

The costs of doing business across the globe—travel, the movement of goods, the sharing of information—have all decreased. The net result has affected our labor economy in two significant ways. First, US-based companies have moved jobs to lower-cost labor markets overseas, a practice known as offshoring. Historically, this has happened with manufacturing jobs. Between 2001 and 2014, over sixty thousand American factories closed.[6] The heating and air-conditioning company Carrier drew national attention in 2020 for closing one of its Indiana factories over presidential objections in favor of bolstering production in its Mexico facility. The quintessential American motorcycle company Harley-Davidson built a new factory in Bangkok, Thailand, and shut the one in Kansas City. Increasingly, we are even seeing more and more service jobs (especially in technology) become vulnerable to offshoring. As recently as 2011, 13 percent of computer programming jobs in the US had moved overseas, mostly to markets like India, China, or Eastern Europe.[7] In total, during the first decade of this century, the US Department of Commerce estimated that 2.4 million jobs were moved overseas.[8]

In addition to American business expanding outward, the availability of lower-skilled immigrant labor coming into our country puts downward price pressure on lower-skilled jobs. Between 1990 and 2007, the number of working-age immigrants in the United States with less than a high school degree more than doubled to almost 18 million people, nearly 10 percent of the working-age population in America.[9]

I am not arguing that either globalization or increased immigrant labor has a net negative impact on our economy. In fact, it could be quite the opposite. The proliferation of offshoring may have given rise to jobs in other sectors, creating new jobs for American workers. A May 2012 paper from economists Gianmarco Ottaviano, Giovanni Peri, and Greg C. Wright found a "productivity effect" from offshoring. They claim that "the cost savings associated with employing . . . offshore labor increases the efficiency of the production process, thus raising the demand for native workers—if not in the same tasks that are offshored . . . then certainly in tasks that are complementary to them."[10] Similarly, studies have shown that an influx of immigrant labor does not, in aggregate, cause wages or employment to go down.[11]

I am also not arguing that globalization or more immigrants with less than a high school education is keeping the floor low on wages because their work is of any less value to our economy. More accurately, I believe it is our collective willingness to value foreign and immigrant labor less—and to exploit this labor—that keeps the floor on wages low.

Clete reflects on his first parish assignment on South Eighteenth Street in Chicago, where his parishioners were primarily Latin American immigrant families. As he got to know them and saw how underpaid and poorly treated they were by employers, he grew angry. This flew in the face of the story we are often told, that America was a "nation of immigrants," a country built by and affirming of immigrants. What he saw in his parish was clear. America was "dishonest about our use of immigrants," Clete said. "We wanted them, but we wanted them cheap. [America was] the shining city, and these immigrants were even willing to put up with [being exploited] because their kids would get born here and then they'd have a chance."

When this broad willingness to exploit the work of immigrants with little education is the American norm, individual businesses are in a pinch. If cheaper labor is available overseas or even within our own borders because of our comfort in paying less for this labor, then increasing wages for those jobs requires an active choice to reduce profits. This is a choice many employers may make, but it is not one the market rewards. So while offshoring and immigration may increase aggregate jobs and even provide for more high-paying jobs, it puts pressure on the lower end of wages, catalyzing further inequality.

## The Decline of Private Sector Labor Unions

Labor unions have long been a means to ensure workers are treated fairly and paid well. By pooling together workers into a larger unit to act as one voice, a union is more powerful than each individual trying to negotiate on their own. If one person asks for a raise, they can easily be ignored. If everyone demands the same raise, managers are more likely to sit down and negotiate.

In America, unions began as a response to industrialization in the late nineteenth century. They often arose as a way to push back against managers and owners who sought to keep wages artificially low or force workers into cheap and unsafe working conditions. Sometimes unions were born out of tragedy. On the afternoon of March 25, 1911, the Triangle shirtwaist factory in New York City caught fire. Scraps of discarded fabric were piled high throughout the factory, and the owners had not installed an alarm system. While the source of the fire is unknown, it spread quickly and workers on the upper floors did not become aware of it until it was too late. One hundred and forty-six workers—mostly immigrant women—were trapped inside and died. It was one of the largest industrial disasters in American history. As a result, the nascent International Ladies' Garment Workers' Union grew rapidly, fighting for safer working conditions to prevent such a tragedy from happening again.

Union ranks grew throughout the early twentieth century as workers fought for better wages and greater safety. By the 1950s, the percentage of American workers who belonged to a union peaked at 35 percent.[12] But then a steady decline began. By 1983, only 20 percent of workers were union members, and by 2015, only 11 percent were.[13] This accelerated drop has been particularly aggressive in the private sector (that is, outside of government jobs like teachers and firefighters), where less than 7 percent of workers are unionized.[14]

Ewan McGaughey from King's College in London has studied the relationship between unionization rates in America and the percentage of our national income the top 1 percent takes home. His review spans a century, from 1910 to 2010. He found that as the number of union members increased, the relative income of the top 1 percent decreased. Conversely, when the number of union members fell, the relative income earned by the top 1 percent rose.[15]

This alone does not prove unions cause income equality. However, many other analyses also suggest a strong relationship. Historian Colin Gordon analyzed wage inequality and unionization rates in all fifty states between 1979 and 2009. He found a clear trend line in each decade: the lower the rates of unionization, the higher the wage inequality.[16] The Bureau of Labor Statistics has shown that between 1983 and 2015, median weekly earnings for nonunion workers consistently trailed those of union members by 20 or 30 percent.[17]

The exact relationship between unionization and wage inequality requires a deeply sophisticated analysis beyond the scope of this book. But the data strongly suggest that the correlation is not accidental. Economists Amanda Gordon and Thomas Lemieux suggest that the decline in unionization may account for one-third of the rise in certain kinds of wage inequality over recent decades.[18]

## The Relationship between Technological Innovation and Educational Attainment

Technology has caused an upheaval in the workplace over the past fifty years. From the proliferation of personal computers in the office to the use of automation on the factory floor, the contemporary workplace looks vastly different from how it did in the 1960s.

A friend of mine who worked at the *Chicago Tribune* for over thirty years tells a story I believe captures this phenomenon quite well. Founded in 1847, the *Tribune* used metal typesetting, first set manually and then by machine, to print the daily newspaper for over a century. By the late 1800s the process required the injection of molten lead into Linotype machines to form the print that would then be set in paragraphs and pages, mass copied, and printed. To operate this complex machinery, well-trained, highly skilled printers were required.

But beginning in the 1970s, computerized photocomposition began replacing the bulky and cumbersome Linotype machines.[19] Fewer human beings were needed to print the newspaper. Those who were needed required vastly different skills.

In 1985, one thousand workers at the *Tribune*, including those of the nation's oldest labor union—the typographical union—went on strike. Management wanted to reassign printers to new roles in the company as their jobs became obsolete. The workers resisted.[20] The resulting strike lasted for forty months, ending in 1987 with an offer for a small buyout of the remaining strikers.[21]

Workers whose technological skills are limited to the current job at hand are hampered in their ability to weather technological innovation. Conversely, workers who are better trained and educated are more able to withstand transitions in the workplace. This is true on two fronts.

First, education develops in people the *specific skills* they need to do new jobs. In the *Tribune* example, when the specific skill of typesetting with a Linotype machine became less needed, a new specific skill to work in computerized layout was more useful. Training and education become critical to working in new technologies.

But perhaps even more important, as Angus Deaton points out, is the relationship between education and the *general skill* of adapting to technological innovation. The more a worker is trained in problem-solving, critical thinking, and the broad array of technological platforms needed in the workforce, the more likely they can adapt to any number of technological changes. The need for higher-level education is particularly true with the rapid acceleration of information technologies in the workplace. Deaton notes, "Better-educated workers can better use new technologies as they come along and are better able to adapt, improve, or tweak new methods."[22]

The result is that those with college degrees are far more likely to transition into and succeed in new types of work as old ones become obsolete. These college graduates are therefore less likely to suffer from economic downturns and can capture value in the form of increased wages.

In the Great Recession from 2008 to 2014, the unemployment rate for those with at least a bachelor's degree peaked at only 5 percent. In contrast, the peak unemployment rate for those with less than a high school degree was three times that: in February 2010, almost 16 percent of workers without a high school diploma were out of work.[23] For workers who were employed in 2014, having a college degree or higher yielded a massive boost to wages: they earned nearly 2.5 times more on average than those with less than a high school degree.[24]

The result is that as technological advancements rapidly revolutionize the workplace, the premium on higher education increases. The gap in employment, wages, and eventually wealth widens between those with higher education and those with less. Research suggests this may only get more pronounced. An Oxford study published in 2013 estimates that 47 percent of US jobs are at risk of disappearing because of automation brought on by technological advances.[25] A later McKinsey study found that if you look at discrete tasks in a job, as opposed to jobs as a whole, as many as 45 percent of the activities American workers perform could become automated.[26] If the future predicted by the Oxford and McKinsey studies plays out, the income and wealth gaps brought on in part by the relationship between education and wages may widen into chasms.

## Family Dynamics

In 1955, when Clete Kiley was only seven years old, Richard J. Daley ran successfully for mayor of Chicago. Mayor Daley's campaign set the tone for his two decades in office until his death in 1976. In a campaign with strong gender (and racial) overtones, Daley sought election as a "Family Man for a Family City." His campaign posters showed pictures of his wife and seven kids. The message was clear. Daley campaigned on a white male-centric economic view of the world: men with families should earn a living wage that enables them to provide for their wives and children at home. This message spoke to Chicagoans. In the fall of 1955, only one-third of all women were in the workforce.[27] Families were reliant on the incomes husbands could bring in.

But between the end of World War II, when women returned from war-sponsored employment to the home, and the early 2000s, women slowly reentered the workforce at a steady rate. In late 2000 and early 2001, we saw a peak of over 60 percent of women in the workforce.[28] Their participation has dipped slightly since then, but in the beginning of 2020, nearly 58 percent of women were still in the workforce—still far more than in the fall of 1955, when Richard Daley was campaigning.[29]

This seismic shift in the makeup of the workforce has intertwined class and gender dynamics to create a compounding effect on wage inequality. Highly educated women and men (who, as we have seen, command higher wages) are more likely to marry each other than they are to marry people with less education. Households with two high-income workers significantly outearn households with two moderate-income workers. And dual-income households at any level often outearn single-income households, particularly single-income households with children.

To illustrate this effect, let's examine the 2014 wage data by income level. Individuals with advanced degrees took home 2.8 times more money per week than individuals with less than a high school degree.[30] But households with two workers with advanced degrees collected three times more per week than households with two workers with less than a high school degree. Week after week after week. Compound that over years. And then pass those effects on to the next generation. The cumulative impact of this household wage gap on wealth inequality becomes quite stark.

We can discern similar effects when we review the rise in single-parent households. In 1960, only 9 percent of children were raised by a single parent. By 2014, 26 percent were.[31] This snapshot of the rise of single-parent households isn't enough to tell us about wage differentials. To do so would require us to at least review how much alimony or child support is paid and compare the adjusted household rates over time. But what we can see is that more and more households are likely to be supported by a single income. These single-parent households undoubtedly earn less on average than households with two income earners.

Collectively, these trends have an enormous impact on inequality. High-income individuals come together to form dual-income households. Their combined earnings far outpace the earnings of low-income individuals forming households. And their earnings further outpace those of the growing number of single-parent households. Compared to a time when most families were supported by the income of a sole male breadwinner, this change in workforce participation has accelerated economic inequality.

## Political Power—Lobbying and Campaign Influence

Social and economic factors have certainly driven top incomes to soar above median incomes. But political factors also play an important role.

The collective lobbying power of corporate interests has grown dramatically over the years. And by "corporate interests," I mean the interests of senior executives and shareholders. In 1971, only 175 businesses kept registered lobbyists in DC. By 1982, just eleven short years later, this number had increased fourteenfold to 2,445.[32] This dramatic increase in lobbying muscle coincides with the sharp rise in inequality that began in the early 1980s. In 1971, when there were only 175 firms retaining registered lobbyists in DC, the statutory corporate tax rate was 48 percent. By 1988, after thousands of businesses retained lobbyists, the corporate tax rate had dipped to 34 percent.[33] But with the implementation of the tax plan Congress passed in 2017, when over 11,000 registered lobbyists worked in DC, it was cut to 21 percent.[34]

Looking at the corporate tax rate is an important lens for understanding economic inequality. Corporate taxes are paid after employees are paid, but before shareholders receive dividends or distributions. This means that the corporate tax rate has no direct impact on employee wages, but it does directly affect shareholders' and executives' equity. The lower the corporate tax rate, the more the owners and top management of a business claim in profits.

It is not just lobbyists who have influence in DC. Wealthy business leaders and their top investors who donate to political campaigns also have a great deal of leverage. In 1964, US political campaigns spent a total of $200 million.[35] By 2012, that number had mushroomed to $6.3 billion. Costs for campaigns have grown faster than the economy as a whole. To fund these costs, a small number of Americans make campaign donations, mostly in small denominations. Fewer than 65,000 Americans—0.02 percent of the population—gave $2,600 or more to political campaigns in 2012.[36] Those giving $2,600 or more are those with the disposable income to do so.

The net result is that elected officials can win elections because their campaigns are funded by the investments of wealthy donors. These wealthy individuals therefore have undue influence on elected leaders. I'm not suggesting a quid pro quo, although that may play out in a limited number of cases. But the need to raise money places elected officials in constant contact with these wealthy individuals. Relationships form. Perspectives are shared. Ideas are influenced. Former Senate majority leader Tom Daschle estimated that US senators spend roughly two-thirds of their time fundraising.[37]

Think about whom you spend two-thirds of your time with. Certainly, their ideas influence your way of thinking.

Undoubtedly one idea held by many wealthy donors is that their taxes should be cut. They relay this idea to elected leaders over phone calls and dinners and drinks. They talk about the benefits of lower tax rates for the rich. They share their economic studies of choice.

But the parishioners and union members Clete works with don't have this access. They aren't meeting with congressional representatives over steak dinners or taking a senator's fundraising phone call. So by mere exposure, our elected leaders aren't getting a balanced view. And this distortion plays out in the policies they enact.

Given that spending on American political campaigns (particularly among the wealthy) dwarfs the political spending in many other democracies, it's no surprise then that the US has one of the lowest marginal tax rates on the wealthy of any developed country.[38] The Organisation for Economic Co-operation and Development (OECD) is a member organization of thirty-six of the most developed economies in the world. In 2018, two-thirds of its member countries had a top marginal tax rate higher than the United States.[39]

Studies have shown that as taxes are cut for the wealthy, income inequality rises. Economists Piketty, Saez, and Stantcheva reviewed the impact of tax cuts on income inequality in eighteen OECD countries between 1960 and 2009. They found that countries that had reduced their top marginal tax rates the most during this period had the greatest increase in national income taken home by the top 1 percent.[40] In this analysis, the United States had slashed its marginal tax rate on top earners more than any other country, save one, and had the highest amount of national income earned by the top 1 percent.

Corporate lobbying muscle and the influence of wealthy campaign donors have increased in the United States for decades. We have simultaneously seen both corporate tax rates and marginal tax rates on individual earners be cut dramatically. These cuts bear a strong relationship to rising inequality when reviewed over four decades and across seventeen similar countries.

## Government Inaction (Drift)

Two political scientists—Jacob Hacker from Yale University and Paul Pierson from the University of California, Berkeley—have outlined a distinct but related relationship between political power and government action they call "drift." They describe it as the "politically driven failure of public policies to adapt to the shifting realities of a dynamic economy."[41] When our legal and political systems don't adapt quickly to the ever-evolving economy, we face drift.

Think about how the government has responded to the growing social media industry. Passed by Congress in 1996, Section 230 of the Communications Decency Act generally provides legal immunity for websites where users post their own content. When it was passed, the idea was that internet service providers like the early company Prodigy should not be held liable for the indecent, fraudulent, or libelous messages that users posted on their message boards. In short, it treated internet service providers more like bookstores (which are generally not liable if a book they sell makes fraudulent claims) and less like publishers (which are more likely liable if they push out criminal claims).

This was just before the social media industry exploded. Facebook was founded eight years after Section 230 was passed, and Twitter was founded ten years after. These platforms didn't exist when Section 230 was passed, but today billions of people use them every month. Despite this massive cultural shift, Section 230 has remained largely unchanged for twenty-five years. This isn't because reforms aren't being discussed. A diverse set of political leaders ranging from Democratic US senator Elizabeth Warren to Republican US senator Ted Cruz have called for greater regulation of these platforms, although they have different solutions in mind. But change hasn't yet come. Certainly, the efforts of giant tech companies and the army of corporate lobbyists they employ to resist change have slowed the process. But even beyond that, the hard work of governing in a democracy—which requires painstaking efforts to build broad coalitions—takes time. It has been easier to develop new technologies and companies than it is to get a majority of the elected representatives of over 300 million Americans to come to a consensus on how to change laws to address the new realities of social media.

The financial world is also prone to drift. In particular, the political scientists Hacker and Pierson point to hedge fund taxation rates as a prime example. Hedge funds raise money from very wealthy individuals to place into complex investments with the potential for high returns. The people who run these funds are called hedge fund managers, and many have become exorbitantly rich. Six of the fifty richest people in the world in 2020 were hedge fund managers.[42] Despite their incredible wealth, the incomes they earn for managing other people's money is qualified as capital gains, which are taxed at 20 percent. Their earnings are not taxed at the rate of ordinary income, which is capped at just under 40 percent. Therefore, the income earned by hedge fund managers is taxed at a lower rate than the income earned by, say, retail store managers (and by almost every other worker). Hacker and Pierson point out that these taxation rules were set long before hedge funds became such a large driver of personal wealth. As recently as 1990, many considered hedge funds a "fringe" investment concept.[43] In 2002, there were only around two thousand of them in existence.[44] But by 2015, that number had quintupled to ten thousand, and the political system hadn't yet adapted to this reality. The government still treats hedge funds exactly the same way it did when such investment companies were rare. Hence government inaction, or drift, has led to income inequality—in this example, by allowing ultrawealthy hedge fund managers to keep more of their income than salaried income earners.

Drift is understandable. It may be driven in part by politicians' interest in keeping donors and powerful constituents happy. But it can also be created by the way our systems are set up. Our economy rewards innovation; those who can make better products at cheaper costs get profits. Our political system, by contrast, rewards the status quo or slow-moving change. A democracy requires the building of coalitions of disparate parties with often competing interests in order for change to happen. As such, our political system will often adapt more slowly than our economic system. A result has been the widening of income and wealth inequality.

—

Returning to the time line of events that unfolded over the course of Father Clete's life, we see how it mirrors the patterns that have fueled the rise of economic inequality. Like many great stories, it takes place over three acts.

In act 1, the United States emerged out of the Great Depression and World War II. We were steeped in our sense of togetherness. We had survived two national traumas by pulling closer to each other, by investing in our country, and by sacrificing as a people. Against this backdrop, it's not hard to see why the CEOs of the early 1960s earned only twenty to thirty times the average worker's salary or how the top 1 percent of Americans took home only 13 percent of the national wealth.

But then, in act 2, dramatic changes unfolded. The Cold War set in. We needed a foil, a reason to continue our aggression against the Soviet Union and to justify our war in Vietnam. Freedom became that value. And what began as a love of political freedom quickly morphed into a cult of economic freedom—of market autonomy. The language of responsibility to and for one another gave way to a heightened form of individualism. Our sense of economic duty to one another faded. We began to hold dear our right to be free from one another.

Act 3 began with us alone on the global field as the victors of the Cold War. Our national narrative was vindicated. A new wave of Clintonian Democrats was ushered in. Like their Republican counterparts, they did not believe in Roosevelt's New Deal or in Johnson-era investments in one another. Instead, they carried with them a "third way," seeking to unleash the power of the markets and market leaders on our country's biggest challenges. In doing so, they cultivated the interests of the wealthy. They did so not based on a Machiavellian political calculus (or at least not just based on a Machiavellian political calculus) but from an assumption that the narrative of the past few decades was right. Political freedom and economic autonomy were the moral campaigns of the day.

Few things are as dangerous as a winner. Victories rarely drive introspection.

Deregulation ramped up. A social safety net that had expanded over three decades to take care of our most vulnerable people was replaced with new laws that sought to remove that burden from those most capable of carrying it. Clinton's 1992 campaign promise to "end welfare as we know it" came to fruition in 1996 as a new welfare regime took hold that limited benefits and required recipients to work. In 1999, Congress repealed the Glass-Steagall Act—the hallmark set of laws from the 1930s that regulated the financial industry to prevent a repeat of the Great Depression—and Clinton signed it into law. Admittedly, Clinton's "third way" was a far cry from the draconian cuts his Republican counterparts sought. But it did mark a clear departure from a more comprehensive view of the government's responsibility to referee the market and protect the most marginalized.

In hindsight, we now know where this all led. Nine years after the repeal of Glass-Steagall, rampant deregulation precipitated the greatest financial collapse in almost a century. The gap between the ultrawealthy and everyone else increased with ferocity. Average workers looked ahead to their future with less optimism for themselves or their children than previous generations had.

The underlying social and economic conditions that permitted our current inequality to take shape are real and true. The rise of globalization and immigration, the decline of labor unions, and disparities in educational attainment hastened the rise of inequality.

Changing family dynamics, the rise of corporate lobbying power, and government inaction also ushered in this new era.

But what Clete's life illuminates is that perhaps an even more powerful force was at play: the force of an enabling national narrative.

As a country we allowed economic inequality to rush forth unchecked because we were in the midst of changing our national narrative. We were no longer convinced that what made us strong and powerful was our interdependence and our commitment to one another. We instead believed that it was our refusal to be bound to one another that set us apart from the rest of the world. As the Soviet Bloc collapsed and we thrived, we took a victory lap—and at breakneck speeds. We played into our worst economic instincts and ferociously deregulated our markets. A civic prosperity gospel took shape: those who could amass wealth were worthy of it, and the role of a freedom-loving government was to remove barriers to the hoarding of wealth. Those who fell behind did so because of their own failings.

As foreign as this new national narrative may have been to leaders who had survived a Depression and a World War—or, as we will see later, to America's Founders—maybe we could survive it if the benefits to our country outweighed the harms. But as we will see, this is just not the case.

# THE HARMS OF
# INEQUALITY

# 5

# ECONOMIC INEQUALITY PUTS PRESSURE ON EVERYDAY AMERICANS

We've seen that our nation is experiencing levels of economic inequality that haven't been seen since before World War II. Our inequality is particularly pronounced along race and gender lines, lines that have been historically unequal.

But does this matter?

For six years of my childhood, my family lived in Germany. My father was stationed there multiple times as an army officer. In our last tour, I was in middle school. My junior high years coincided with a historic shift in the country. We moved to West Germany in 1988. We experienced the collapse of East Germany, which had spent more than forty years as a Soviet-allied Communist country. We witnessed the fall of the Berlin Wall and watched as reunification happened around us. The night before we flew home to the United States for good, my family of four crowded around the TV in a cramped hotel room. The Bundestag had just voted to move the nation's capital from Bonn back to Berlin. Germans were celebrating in the streets.

During this dynamic period, we lived in the Nuremberg area, a little over an hour's drive from the East German border. After the collapse, my German teacher organized an exchange program with a school in the picturesque former–East German town of Oberwiesenthal, on the border of Czechoslovakia. For a week, my classmates and I lived with local families and went to the local school. We sat in on small-town life in this village that was newly opened to the Western world.

I loved the people I met. The host family I stayed with was warm and funny, and the students curious and inviting. I even remember visiting the town's local ski resort, which, if I remember correctly, was famous in the region for its ski jump.

But I also remember the stark contrast I witnessed between Oberwiesenthal and the Bavarian region I had called home for over two years. Everything seemed worn. The construction was drab and monochromatic and ran counter to the vibrant spirit of the people I was getting to know. Cars were functional but dated. Even the clothes of the residents were more muted. While I did not see evidence of absolute poverty, the median standard of living, from all appearances, was much lower than what we had witnessed in towns throughout Bavaria.

I have taken from that the personal belief that forced equality is not a solution. It is impractical at best, tyrannical at worst, and ineffective through and through. I know of no Communist economies from the 1970s that have held onto the bulk of their market restrictions *and* are better off today than they were then.

Cold War Eastern Europe and Soviet Russia had national narratives around the virtue of equality that ultimately impeded their people's abilities to thrive. But today, we in the United States are building up a national narrative around the virtue of *in*equality—a narrative that is holding us back. We tell ourselves that inequality encourages innovation, hard work, and entrepreneurship. By allowing people and corporations to capture extremely large shares of the returns from their work and risk-taking, we encourage that behavior. This, we say, has led to a rising tide, which lifts all boats in our country.

When we reward risk and allow people to capture the benefits of their hard work, we are ensuring more risk-taking and hard work. But the accompanying inequality we have created does not always coincide with economic advancement. American economist Heather Boushey says, "We have to get rid of the false story that we need to create inequality to grow the economy."[1] Forcing disproportionate inequality is not necessary for economic growth. We have already seen that it wasn't so in the 1950s and 1960s, when we had far less inequality and our economy grew at a pace we envy today. It isn't true now.

Acknowledging that economic inequality isn't necessary for economic growth is a start. We must go further, though, and come to terms with how economic inequality is corroding the foundation of our country.

———

Walking around Harlem with Jamaal Nelson is a bit like having a fawning docent shepherd me through a beloved museum.[2] It is a spring afternoon and the warm air, sunny sky, and budding blooms on the trees all seem to chase away months of winter. The two of us have gotten to know each other while working together to inspire teachers around the country to become more politically active. We have a few hours to kill between meetings, and having Jamaal show me around his neighborhood sounds like a great way to spend the time.

As a preacher and a political organizer, Jamaal is steeped in storytelling. Each building and park comes with a story. This church had a scandal a few years back. This is the best place to grab a burger. This nightclub held some great parties during the Harlem Renaissance. This park is where kids used to avoid playing because of gang activity; it is safer now. It's not a predetermined trail so much as a scavenger hunt, with each stop reminding Jamaal of a nearby place he wants to show me. And his eyes light up with delight at so many turns.

Jamaal has lived in Harlem with few gaps since the early 2000s. But he was born and raised in Soundview, in the Bronx. His father grew up in a Gullah-speaking community in South Carolina. "He told stories of picking cotton and his mother picking cotton and his mother's mother being a slave," Jamaal remembers. I am not sure the years add up, but in a community as tight-knit and intergenerationally stable as theirs in the deep South, I am not surprised his family can identify the last person in their ancestry who was enslaved. His father grew up "dirt poor," and could sit in his home and peer outside through the holes in the wall. His mother, also from South Carolina, was the daughter of a railroad worker, so her family had a TV and a car and lived a much more blue-collar life than his dad's family.

Jamaal's parents didn't know each other in South Carolina, but they both followed the patterns of the Great Migration to New York. Jamaal's father served in Vietnam before following his brothers to the city. Jamaal's mother trailed after cousins on the same route. They met, married, and settled in the South Bronx, giving birth to three boys in ten years.

The early part of Jamaal's childhood was stable and secure. His mother was a clerk of the court, and his father worked in the correctional system, first at Sing Sing and then at a smaller facility.

Life was church and school and Sunday drives to Westchester for groceries. But all that changed when Jamaal was eight years old and his mother decided to go back to college, and eventually to medical school. She remembered the cold, clinical way that a doctor had told her family that her own mother passed, leaving her siblings and her father confused in their grief. She knew she could do better with her future patients.

Scarcity took hold of their lives. Down to one income but with student expenses and three boys to raise, Jamaal's parents were under incredible financial stress.

Growing up, Jamaal recounts, "I had three thoughts about money. One, if you have money, you probably wouldn't fight. Two, if you have money, you could eat whatever you want to eat. And three, if you had money, you had options about what to do." Food was scarce. New clothes were rare. Eviction notices piled up and bill collectors began calling the house.

His parents took Jamaal out of Catholic school and placed him in the local public school. "I was a terrible student," Jamaal shares. "If I could have failed out of middle school, I would have failed out." It wasn't until later that he was diagnosed with severe dyslexia. "But I worked like the dickens." And he had drive.

His hard work and some good fortune landed Jamaal at the famed LaGuardia High School of Music & Art and Performing Arts (the selective New York City high school popularized by the movie and TV series *Fame*). Every day, Jamaal rode two trains for over an hour each way to get to school. He had a wonderful speech teacher, trained at Julliard, who molded Jamaal's speech into the deep, resonant voice of a preacher. If you could drink carbonated molasses, that is what Jamaal's voice sounds like. It is rich and smooth and effervescent all at the same time. He got into drama and found it was something he was good at. It also improved his confidence. By the time Jamaal was a senior, he was student body president and preparing to go to Vanderbilt University on a scholarship.

But Vanderbilt was as different from LaGuardia as Nashville is from the Bronx. In the fall of 1995, Jamaal took a Greyhound bus down to Tennessee with his sheets and clothes and a laptop that a friend had purchased for him. When he arrived, he saw other students "with moving trucks and trailers. They would put their beds on stilts so they could put stuff under it. They had so much stuff they had to put their beds on stilts." The campus was green and the buildings were white. Students wore the unofficial uniform of khakis, a button-down, and a fleece. Jamaal, with his jeans and sneakers, stuck out. "An early memory is walking down the perimeter of the campus and everyone would say hello to me. And you only say hello to a stranger in New York because the other person is compromised mentally," Jamaal recalls. *"Everyone here is crazy,"* he remembers thinking.

But just like at LaGuardia, he dove in. He was determined to continue his successful run in student politics and decided he wanted to be elected freshman class senator. For his campaign, he stood in front of the cafeteria shaking hands every night, introducing himself to students. During this time, Colin Powell was coming to campus to speak, and a flyer for the event promoted the talk by posing the question "Can Colin Powell be president?" Someone took the poster, crossed out "Colin Powell" and wrote "a black man." They then drew a person hanging with a noose around his neck and put the poster on Jamaal's door. This scared him to death, but he pushed forward. Jamaal won that election and many others. Eventually, he served as the student body president at Vanderbilt—an election win so remarkable, it was written about in the *New York Times*.[3]

His love of politics and his deep spiritual grounding sent him to Harvard for divinity school and eventually back to New York. By that time, his parents had moved an hour north of the city to

Rockland County so his mother could open her medical practice there. Jamaal's first jobs required splitting his time between a church in Rockland County and Harlem, where he worked as a political organizer. He drove that commute so frequently, there were times he slept in his car.

The distance between the two communities was more than geographic though. It was a journey between two American realities. In Harlem, people were worrying about the quality of their schools, the crime in their neighborhood, and city services that never reached them. "I heard people tell me about babies being sick, the mom calling 9-1-1, and the ambulance not coming. Or running out of baby food, but not going to the corner store because there had been a shooting the night before. Or running out of insulin and being afraid to go to the clinic." In contrast, the families in Rockland County were not stressing about their basic needs being met or their safety.

But more than this, he saw as he got older that his friends from Vanderbilt and Harvard had access to more capital and had fewer financial concerns than his peers and stakeholders in Harlem. "So much of this is intergenerational," Jamaal came to realize. "The passage of wealth from one generation to the next is only being compounded and reinforced." As Jamaal saw it, there were two drivers of this widening gap. One was that the children of rich people had greater access to capital. They could buy a home with their parents contributing the down payment, or start a business by taking out a loan backed by assets they inherited from their parents. In addition, the children of wealthy people inherited a greater understanding of money and how it worked. The combination of both resulted in "the whole idea of [an American] meritocracy being eroded."

As the rich got richer—or their wealth was inoculated from too much loss—everybody else struggled more. It fed a cycle that increased the inequality.

—

Let's start by painting a picture of how many Americans experience inequality in their daily lives. We have seen how stagnant or declining income and rising inequality place a ceiling on what Americans earn. But look down, and we see a fast-moving floor of debt and expenses rising. As income has plateaued for most Americans, basic household expenses such as health care, housing, and childcare keep going up. The result is what I think of as the "great squeeze."

Take a look at health care. Over the past fifty years, the health care industry has grown faster than the economy as a whole, as measured by the gross domestic product (GDP). In 1973, we spent 7 percent of our GDP on health care costs. By 2018, we devoted 18 percent to it.[4] And as the industry is eating up more of society's costs, Americans' incomes are rising far more slowly. The result is that health care costs are taking up more of a household's budget than in the past. In 1973, Americans spent 6 percent of their household budgets on out-of-pocket health care costs.[5] By 2018, that had grown to 8 percent.[6] For low-income families, the picture has been even worse. In the past twenty years alone, the bottom fifth of households have seen their health care costs rise from 17 percent to 22 percent of their income.[7]

The rise in housing costs has similarly outpaced income growth. In 1973, the average home was purchased for three times the amount of the median family income. By 2017, it took five times the median family income to do so.[8]

If basic costs like health care and housing are increasing, are most Americans saving money on other necessities? The short answer is no. The United States Department of Labor collects and publishes annual data on consumer spending—the Consumer Expenditure Survey. By comparing similar spending categories over time, we can see how basic spending needs are eating up more and more of families' budgets.

Let's examine spending across four areas I think of as "basic needs": food, housing, health care, and transportation. In 1999, the bottom fifth of households spent much more than their income on these areas of basic need.[9] This meant discretionary items like entertainment, education, or clothing had to be financed out of debt or savings. By contrast, the top fifth of households only spent 42 percent of their annual income that year on these basic needs, leaving the majority of their income to be spent on discretionary items, invested, or saved.

As wide as this discrepancy was in 1999, it has only gotten worse since. For families in the bottom bracket, these basic needs were eating up an even higher percentage of their income in 2018 than they had in 1999 (Figure 8). But for the top bracket, the percentage

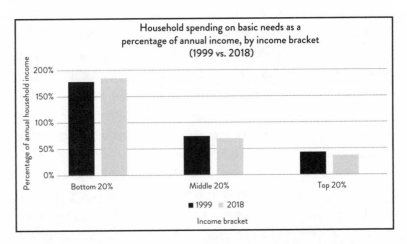

Figure 8. *Source:* "Consumer Expenditures in 1999," US Bureau of Labor Statistics, May 2001, table 1, https://www.bls.gov/cex/csxann99.pdf; "Consumer Expenditures in 2018," US Bureau of Labor Statistics, last modified May 2020, table B, https://www.bls.gov/opub/reports/consumer-expenditures/2018/home.htm.

of their income they devoted to these costs went down during the same period.[10] Middle-income households saw a slight decline in the percentage of their income spent on these basic expenses, but not as strong a decline as the top-income families experienced.

One final area I want to call out is childcare. Even though the Consumer Expenditure Surveys do not specifically report childcare costs, as a parent I can attest that this is a major part of many families' budgets. As in other areas of basic needs, we see a similar trend of childcare costs rising faster than household income. For women who paid for childcare in 1988, the average monthly costs equaled 7 percent of their income.[11] By 2011, those costs had grown to 10 percent.[12]

The costs of basic needs like health care, housing, and childcare are rising faster than most wages are rising. As more of their income is being eaten up by basic needs, middle- and low-income American households are losing the ability to invest in their futures.

Looking at how Americans' savings habits have changed over time illustrates how many families are feeling the squeeze. For most years between 1959 and 1980, the personal savings rates for American households hovered between 10 and 15 percent. In the mid-1980s, this began to decline steadily, hitting a record low of 2 percent in July 2005. In July 2019, it sat at 7 percent.[13] As a result of such low savings, the Federal Reserve reports that 40 percent of Americans couldn't cover a $400 emergency expense.[14]

Jamaal has felt this in his own life. He shares, "There is this tremendous squeeze. If you look at [my family's] income, you would say, 'Golly, Jamaal, you do super well. Solid middle class.' And yet, the cost of living is just so explosive." The crisis is exacerbated for the poor and the working class. "Just think about folks who don't have even the economic privilege I have," Jamaal adds. "These are folks who are stuck, perpetually underemployed or unemployed.

The debt that they've got to rack up [just to pay basic expenses]. The system really is built to prey upon the lower classes and middle class. Their debt in many ways is feeding the wealth of the top 1 percent."

As Jamaal sees it, the great squeeze is not only a by-product of rising inequality but a driver of it. The great squeeze *feeds* inequality. We have a "struggling middle class," Jamaal points out, but unfortunately, the national narrative about autonomy and responsibility hasn't changed. "For the wealthy, we say take the money you have inherited and keep living cool," but for everyone else, the message remains "live beneath your means, save to invest in assets." In fact, it is almost as if we are moving the goalposts for the middle class and the working poor.

What Jamaal points to is something akin to what French economist Thomas Piketty notes in his groundbreaking best seller *Capital in the Twenty-First Century*. Through his research, Piketty uncovers that in contemporary Western countries, slowing economic growth has resulted in returns on capital being higher than income growth. Or put another way, having money makes you richer than working for money does.

Piketty believes that in many countries, average returns on capital (e.g., business profits, stock dividends, and real estate appreciation) will remain between 4 and 5 percent per year, while economic growth will continue to lag behind at 1 to 1.5 percent.[15] When this happens year over year and decade over decade, those who have inherited money will earn more on their wealth than most Americans who build their wealth from their labor earn on theirs. This means the benefit of having been rich yesterday (or having had rich parents or grandparents) is greater than the benefit of working hard today. Because our economy returns more to those whose wealth was accrued at some point in the past than it does to those who work to amass wealth today, Piketty sums up the phenomenon as "the past devours the future."[16]

When you layer this phenomenon on top of what we have already seen—rising costs and stagnating wages—it is nearly impossible for the average American to buy into the cycle of wealth. The story that if people "work hard and play by the rules," as President Clinton put it in his 1992 presidential campaign, they can grab hold of the American dream is becoming less and less true. Our economy rewards being rich more than working hard. And some Americans are beginning to notice.

As Jamaal's circumstances changed, it appeared to him that the rules also continued to change. In the community where he grew up, he was told, "If you rent an apartment, that's good enough." But as he moved in different circles, he learned the message there was "No, you need a house." Once, he thought the secret to financial prosperity was landing a high-paying job. Now he has learned that "the secret to wealth is accruing assets that throw off money for you."

But it gets harder and harder to get there. When costs keep rising faster than income, people lose the ability to save, which prevents them from investing in stocks or real estate to accrue wealth. The middle class can't buy into the wealth-creating cycle, so the inequality gap keeps growing.

Americans are no longer "rewarded by the sweat of our brow," Jamaal concludes. Getting wealthy "is really about being in the club, which very often intersects with race, with whiteness. If you're in the club, you have a much easier time achieving wealth irrespective of how hard you work." What he doesn't say, but is understood, is that if you are outside of the club, no matter how hard you work, the dream of achieving wealth will continue to fade into the distance.

This is the tragedy of the great squeeze in a world where wealth is determined more and more by capital and less by income.

—

American families are feeling this squeeze. They can't afford the same level of basic essentials they could thirty years ago. They save less. They feel at risk of financial setback or even calamity should an unplanned expense creep up.

Yet they see the GDP growing and sense that the rich are just getting richer. This dissonance tears at the sense that we are Americans bound together across differences. This places our society at a dangerous precipice: we are teetering over and looking down upon an irreparably divided country.

When we zoom out from the perspective of an individual family, we see economic inequality waging a war on our national well-being on multiple fronts. This inequality coincides with a broad range of social ills and challenges the social fabric our democracy needs to thrive. It also runs counter to one of our most fundamental American values: that it is the collective strength across our differences that makes us uniquely American. Let's spend the next three chapters understanding the assaults on our country's future on each of these fronts.

# 6

# ECONOMIC INEQUALITY POISONS OUR SOCIAL WELL-BEING

Mike Espinoza from Houston tells the story of Beto from his old neighborhood. "Beto was kind of an OG," an "original gangster." "He got locked up and spent something like five years inside. Before he went away, his wife had become pregnant, so he didn't meet his daughter for nearly five years."

In prison, Beto found God and became a Christian. It changed his life. When he got out, he joined Mike's dad's church and became a kind of neighborhood evangelist. "He gave me and my brother the hardest sermon because we were the preacher's kid, and yet we were out in the street."

When not at the church or at home, Beto worked at a warehouse in a large industrial area on the east side of Houston. "He worked with another OG from another neighborhood who was still in the street life," Mike remembers. This coworker murdered Beto at the worksite, impaling him with a forklift.

Beto's murder sent shock waves through the community. "This guy got out. He changed his life. He was living for Christ. He was working hard to support his baby. Then his past came back to haunt him. You try to do good, but bad shit still happens." Mike pauses. "I remember wondering, *Can we ever really get out of this? Are we ever really free?*"

Beto's story illustrates how economic inequality fuels unhealthy communities. Good individual choices matter, sure. But would he have been murdered if the community he grew up in had a greater share of the resources and wealth of our incredibly rich nation? There is no way to know for certain, but the research suggests it may have been less likely. After all, we can extol the virtues of decency and hard work and clean living. But if we still subject communities to the public health risks of economic inequality, no one can ever really be free.

———

Does more money make a community healthier? To a certain extent, it does, but only up to a point. Richard Wilkinson and Kate Pickett's powerful book *The Spirit Level* examines the limits of this relationship between national wealth and social benefits. They uncover a strong trend between national wealth and positive outcomes such as life expectancy and happiness.[1] But here is the interesting thing. Beginning at a national per-capita income of about $20,000, the trend starts to wane. When per-capita income reaches $30,000 and above, there is almost no relationship at all between more national wealth and higher life expectancy or greater happiness within society. However, among the higher-earning countries, what *is* positively correlated to many better social outcomes is the degree of income equality. That is, once a country attains a certain level of prosperity, economic equality often becomes a better predictor of social well-being than wealth.

Wilkinson and Pickett have outlined several societal outcomes that play out differently in Organisation for Economic Co-operation and Development (OECD) countries and in various US states depending on the level of inequality. The impact of inequality on crime and punishment, public health, and education is frightening.

## Crime and Punishment

Let's start with where the Beto story points us. In unequal rich countries, the homicide rate (homicides per million people per year) can be triple that of the homicide rate in more equal rich countries (Figure 9). Even when you eliminate an outlier like the United States (whose homicide rate exceeds an astonishingly high level of sixty murders per million people), we see this correlation between inequality and homicides play out. An unequal country like Portugal, for example, has a homicide rate approaching forty homicides per million. On the other end of the spectrum, more equal countries like Norway and Japan experience fewer than ten per million.

Fascinatingly, this same trend plays out within the United States. States with high income inequality far outpace the national average when it comes to homicides per million people (Figure 10). More equal states (like Utah, New Hampshire, and Iowa) have rates that come much closer to the rates seen in more equal countries (like Japan, Norway, and Sweden.)

It's worth pointing out here that Wilkinson and Pickett concede that correlation does not necessarily prove causation for these or any of their data.[2] That is, the fact that two factors (like homicides and inequality) are often found together does not mean that one necessarily causes the other. But when similar trends manifest across multiple social outcomes in comparisons with other nations and between US states, the overall pattern suggests that a strong

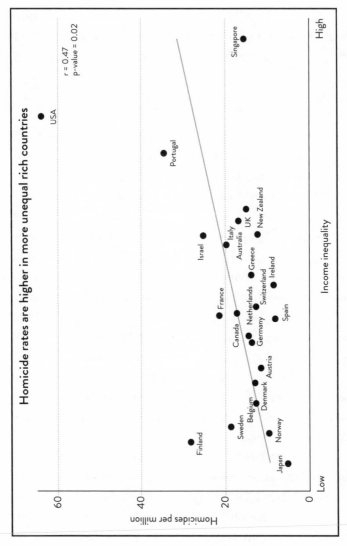

Figure 9. *Source:* Richard Wilkinson and Kate Pickett, *The Spirit Level: Why Greater Equality Makes Societies Stronger* (New York: Bloomsbury, 2010), 135, quoted in "The Spirit Level," The Equality Trust, accessed March 25, 2021, https://www.equalitytrust.org.uk/resources/the-spirit-level.

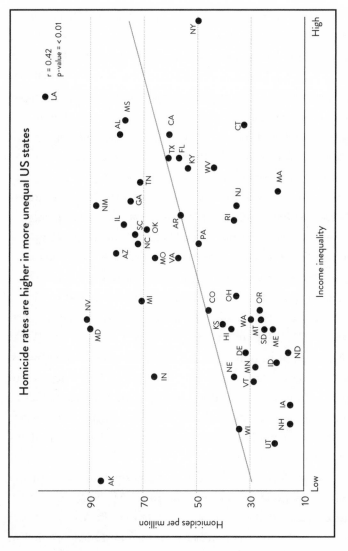

Figure 10. *Source:* Richard Wilkinson and Kate Pickett, *The Spirit Level: Why Greater Equality Makes Societies Stronger* (New York: Bloomsbury, 2010), 136, quoted in "The Spirit Level," The Equality Trust, accessed March 25, 2021, https://www.equalitytrust.org.uk/resources/the-spirit-level.

relationship of some kind exists between economic inequality and homicide rates.

Looking beyond the single crime of murder, we see that criminal punishment is doled out more often in unequal rich countries. In a review of the United Nations *Survey on Crime Trends and the Operations of Criminal Justice Systems*, Wilkinson and Pickett found that unequal rich countries imprisoned nearly eight times the number of prisoners per one hundred thousand people than more equal countries (Figure 11).

In the United States, we see the same trend play out across states. More unequal states imprison twice as many people per one hundred thousand residents as more equal ones (Figure 12).

There are undoubtedly a host of reasons for this gap in incarceration rates. One could be that crime rates are simply higher in more unequal countries and states. Higher inequality might inspire more crime. The difference in homicide rates lends credence to this argument. Another reason could be that attitudes toward policing and a general level of mistrust in unequal societies lead to higher incarceration rates regardless of the underlying crime rates. In fact, Wilkinson and Pickett found in a review of the European and World Values Survey that in rich countries and across the United States, citizens in less equal areas trust one another less. What appears to be clear from the research is that incarceration rates are higher in more unequal rich countries and states. Underlying crime rates, attitudes toward the police, and a higher distrust of fellow residents all combine to contribute to this.

It is impossible to talk about incarceration rates, particularly in America, without acknowledging race. Michelle Alexander, a law professor and the respected author of *The New Jim Crow*, which explores the intersection between race and incarceration in America, notes that "research has shown the most punitive nations are the most diverse."[3] In the United States, the NAACP reports

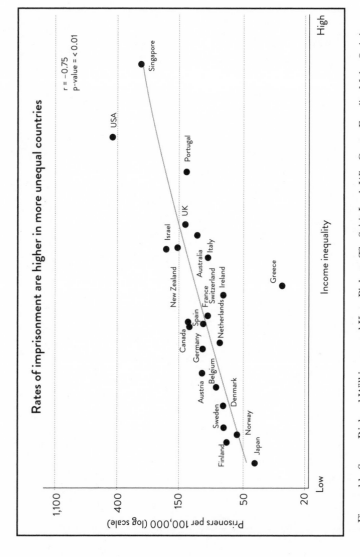

Figure 11. *Source:* Richard Wilkinson and Kate Pickett, *The Spirit Level: Why Greater Equality Makes Societies Stronger* (New York: Bloomsbury, 2010), 148, quoted in "The Spirit Level," The Equality Trust, accessed March 25, 2021, https://www.equalitytrust.org.uk/resources/the-spirit-level.

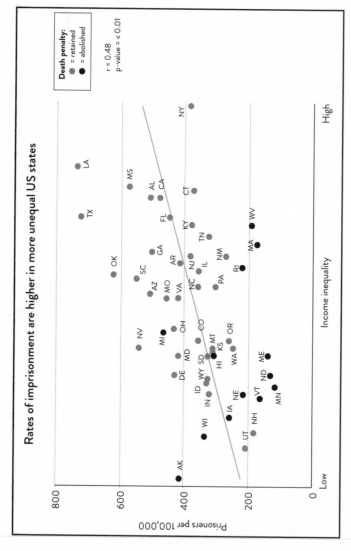

Figure 12. *Source: Richard Wilkinson and Kate Pickett, The Spirit Level: Why Greater Equality Makes Societies Stronger* (New York: Bloomsbury, 2010), 149, quoted in "The Spirit Level," The Equality Trust, accessed March 25, 2021, https://www.equalitytrust.org.uk/resources/the-spirit-level.

that Black Americans are incarcerated at five times the rate of white Americans.[4] Race plays an enormous role, along with income inequality, in leading to increased incarceration rates.

## Public Health

High homicide rates and mass incarceration don't tend to concentrate in otherwise healthy societies. Let's dig even deeper and explore public health. Economist Angus Deaton explores how wealth—on a societal level—has had a powerful impact on life expectancy historically. Prior to 1750, for example, the families of high-status nobility in England had the same life expectancy as the general population. But beginning in 1750, life expectancies for these two groups began to diverge.

Noble families began to live far longer, on average, than their lower-class countrymen. By roughly 1850, these families had an average life expectancy at birth that was 50 percent higher than the general population.[5] So what happened? Between 1750 and 1850, England underwent tremendous changes in terms of knowledge development and innovation. Improved nutrition, better sanitation, and medical innovations (particularly vaccination and germ theory) all played a huge role in the rapid increase in life expectancy among these ducal families. The good news is that as these innovations became standardized, they rolled out across broader society. The wealthy benefitted first, then the general population. Today, members of noble families don't live 50 percent longer than the general population. The innovations and knowledge that first became available to the wealthy eventually made their way to most everyone else.

We have seen this pattern play out on the international level as well. In 1950, life expectancy in northern Europe was thirty years longer than it was in most of Asia. In Asian countries, people lived on average to only their midforties (or below). But by 2010, life expectancies had increased to midfifties in South Asia, to over sixty in Southeast Asia, and to nearly seventy in East Asia.[6] The reasons for these increases are largely the same as in England two centuries ago: the rapid scaling up of medical innovations, the stabilization of food supply systems, and increased sanitation.

But just as we have begun to see, there are limits to the benefits of having more wealth. After a while, wealth concentrated at the top no longer drives public health innovation that all can benefit from. After a while, inequality may make a society sicker.

Let's start at birth. In more unequal countries, we see much higher infant mortality rates. In the United States, for example, for every one thousand babies born, nearly seven will die before their first birthday.[7] Our infant mortality rate is *twice* that of Japan and Sweden, where fewer than three out of every one thousand children will die in their first year. In fact, depressingly, among 19 similarly developed countries, the United States has the highest infant mortality rate (Figure 13).[8]

Mental health is also affected. The World Health Organization established the World Mental Health Survey Consortium in 1998 to further understand and address the "global burden of mental disorders."[9] Through this consortium, face-to-face interviews are conducted on a representative sample of participants in twenty-seven countries, collecting information on a wide variety of disorders. Wilkinson and Pickett compared the results from the World Mental Health Survey for the nine countries in the OECD for which they had the most extensive data on income inequality. They uncovered a strong trend that shows more reported mental illness in more unequal countries (Figure 14).

Inequality appears to affect drug use in a society as well. Beginning in 2007, the United States Office on Drugs and Crime began

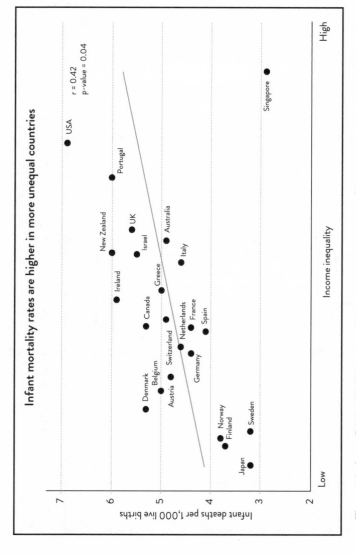

Figure 13. *Source:* Richard Wilkinson and Kate Pickett, *The Spirit Level: Why Greater Equality Makes Societies Stronger* (New York: Bloomsbury, 2010), 82, quoted in "The Spirit Level," The Equality Trust, accessed March 25, 2021, https://www.equalitytrust.org.uk/resources/the-spirit-level.

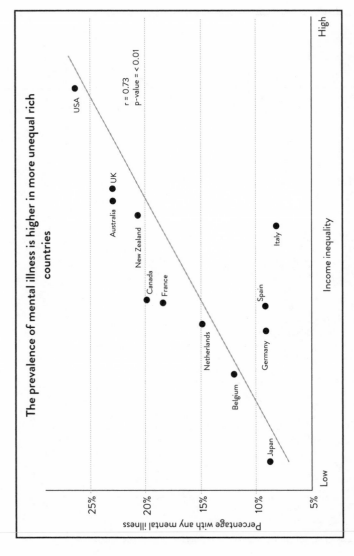

Figure 14. *Source:* Richard Wilkinson and Kate Pickett, *The Spirit Level: Why Greater Equality Makes Societies Stronger* (New York: Bloomsbury, 2010), 67, quoted in "The Spirit Level," The Equality Trust, accessed March 25, 2021, https://www.equalitytrust.org.uk/resources/the-spirit-level.

publishing a *World Drug Report*, in which countries share information on drug supply and drug demand. In reviewing the 2007 *World Drug Report*, Wilkinson and Pickett looked at rates of usage for a variety of addictive substances such as opiates, cannabis, cocaine, MDMA, and amphetamines. They combined the use of these drugs into a single index, then compared the results across nearly two dozen OECD countries. They found a clear trend: in countries with more income inequality, illegal drug usage was higher (Figure 15).

Obesity rates are also higher in more unequal rich countries: two and a half times higher, according to Wilkinson and Pickett's analysis of data from the World Obesity Federation. In the United States, over 30 percent of adults are obese. In more equal countries like Norway and Sweden, the obesity rates are closer to 10 percent. Japan, a true outlier with among the lowest rates of income inequality, had an obesity rate under 4 percent (Figure 16).[10]

Admittedly, inequality isn't the sole cause of all these negative public health outcomes. National variations in diet and exercise may help explain part of the difference in obesity rates. I would imagine different cultural attitudes toward drugs also affect the rates at which people use narcotics. But when infant mortality, mental illness, drug use, and obesity all show up more frequently in more unequal societies, it seems clear that there is a link between public health and inequality.

These public health factors add up. Inequality, it seems, brings down life expectancy in rich countries. In a review of life expectancy among highly developed nations, individuals in unequal countries lived three years less than their peers in more equal ones. The United States, with the second-highest rate of income inequality in the study, had an average life expectancy that was five years less than that of Japan, whose rates of income inequality are among the lowest (Figure 17).

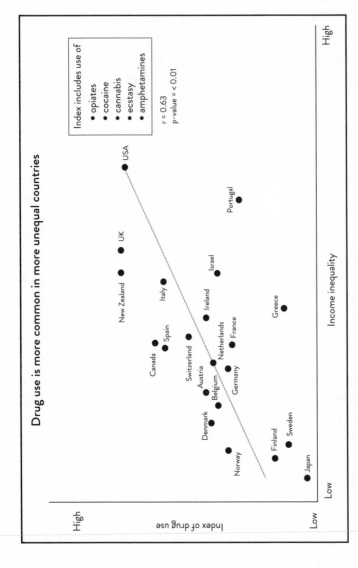

Figure 15. *Source:* Richard Wilkinson and Kate Pickett, *The Spirit Level: Why Greater Equality Makes Societies Stronger* (New York: Bloomsbury, 2010), 71, quoted in "The Spirit Level," The Equality Trust, accessed March 25, 2021, https://www.equalitytrust.org.uk/resources/the-spirit-level.

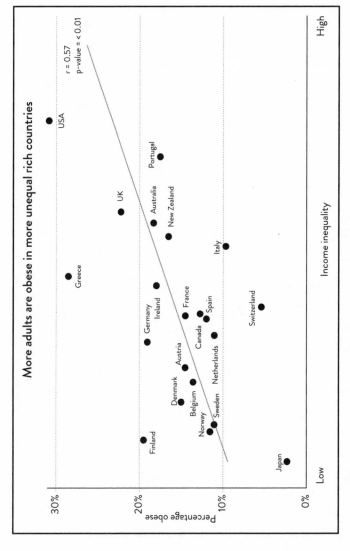

Figure 16. *Source:* Richard Wilkinson and Kate Pickett, *The Spirit Level: Why Greater Equality Makes Societies Stronger* (New York: Bloomsbury, 2010), 92, quoted in "The Spirit Level," The Equality Trust, accessed March 25, 2021, https://www.equalitytrust.org.uk/resources/the-spirit-level.

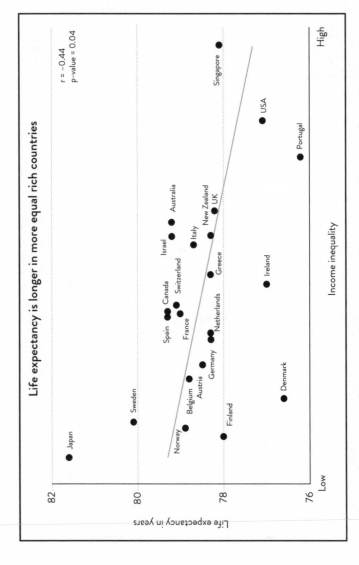

Figure 17. *Source:* Richard Wilkinson and Kate Pickett, *The Spirit Level: Why Greater Equality Makes Societies Stronger* (New York: Bloomsbury, 2010), 82, quoted in "The Spirit Level," The Equality Trust, accessed March 25, 2021, https://www.equalitytrust.org.uk/resources/the-spirit-level.

It is better for your health to live in a slightly less rich but more equal country than it is to live in a richer country with greater inequality, such as the United States. When a society's people are more mentally ill, more addicted, less healthy, and more frequently murdered, they tend to live shorter lives.

The same phenomenon plays out when reviewing states in the US. Those with the highest degree of income inequality have life expectancies that are on average two years shorter than the states with the lowest degree of income inequality.[11]

When all the data are compiled, we must acknowledge the tragic fact that the poorest Americans can now expect to live ten to fifteen fewer years than the wealthiest.[12] In a land where we are taught that "all men are created equal," rich people are created more equal. The price of poverty is unacceptably high for the poor—up to, on average, fifteen years of their lives. And the price of that poverty in an otherwise wealthy nation is, on so many dimensions, tragically high.

Before we move on, I want to call out once again the impact race plays here. Just as we saw wage and wealth inequality magnified when viewed through a racial lens, we see the same pattern play out with life expectancy. In 2006, life expectancy for Black men was six years less than that of white men; for Black women, it was four years less than for white women.[13] The price of poverty and race, when put together, weighs heavily on our country.

## Educational Attainment

Twenty-two years ago, I took a job that would change my life. Situated on a grassy field near the intersection of Acadian Thruway and Winbourne Avenue on the north side of Baton Rouge, Dalton Elementary School would teach me more about my country than any of the six public schools I had attended as a child. Weeks prior to my first day as a teacher, I was 1,300 miles away, casually attending lectures on a comfortably warm campus dotted with green lawns and Gothic buildings. But during those last weeks in August of 1999, in heat that pressed on a person the whole day, I stood in front of two dozen Black five-year-olds navigating everything from how they would learn to read to who could use the restroom when.

In short time, I fell in love with the community of Dalton Elementary. My students were dynamic, curious, and filled with enough energy and spit to both drive me crazy and make me laugh. Experienced teachers showed me how to teach well and discipline firmly, always grounded in love. Our elderly janitor came to school early every morning just to open up the building so I could get in before everyone else. Our principal suffered few fools: she was kind and tough, telling me to change what I was doing when it wasn't working and smiling at me in the halls when she saw me catching on. And the families, all Black parents and grandparents and aunties, showed me—a white northerner fresh out of college—patience and grace as they worked with me to teach their children.

But this school so full of goodness sat immersed in a larger society whose toxicity seeped in every day. Broken windowpanes in my classroom were replaced with opaque plastic that grew dingy brown with age. I had few books, let alone textbooks, for my kids. We had a nurse who would come only twice a month. If you walked out the school doors and drove around the neighborhood, you saw a community whose natural wealth had been stolen over generations. Housing was inconsistent, meaning some of my students bounced from place to place. Jobs were scarce, forcing many parents to take public transportation to the white side of town for work. The fifth-largest oil refinery in America sat just over a mile from my school. When my students got sick, there were few doctors on the north side of town that could see them.

Surrounded by all this brokenness, Dalton's academic scores were low and its discipline problems were high. The love of our families, dynamism of our students, and tirelessness of our teachers all combined to shoulder that Sisyphean boulder up the hill. But it kept rolling back.

The story of Dalton Elementary school in north Baton Rouge is not unique.

One of the most common and reliable measurements of educational attainment across countries is the Programme for International Student Assessment (PISA). Founded in 1997 and operated by OECD, it measures math, science, and literacy performance among fifteen-year-olds. In 2015, PISA measured results from over half a million students in seventy-two countries.

What Wilson and Pickett found in reviewing PISA's 2003 data was a strong correlation between income equality and higher math and literacy scores. They saw a similar trend mirrored for adult literacy when reviewing the results from the International Adult Literacy Survey (Figure 18).

When they narrowed their focus to the United States, a parallel trend played out. The 2003 math and reading scores from eighth grade students showed some important variability, but the trend line was clear. More unequal states had lower scores than more equal states. Carry this forward to high school, and we see a correlation between income inequality and a failure to graduate. Less equal states have dropout rates that exceed 25 percent, while more equal ones have rates below 15 percent (Figure 19).

After my time in Dalton, I worked in public education for nearly two decades. I have worked in homogeneous schools like Dalton, where 100 percent of students are Black and come from low-income families. I have worked in incredibly diverse schools, where 50 percent of students are children of color and 50 percent come from low-income families. I can attest that demography is not destiny.

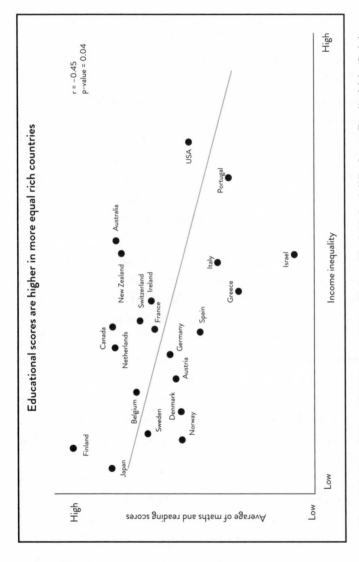

Figure 18. *Source:* Richard Wilkinson and Kate Pickett, *The Spirit Level: Why Greater Equality Makes Societies Stronger* (New York: Bloomsbury, 2010), 106, quoted in "The Spirit Level," The Equality Trust, accessed March 25, 2021, https://www.equalitytrust.org.uk/resources/the-spirit-level.

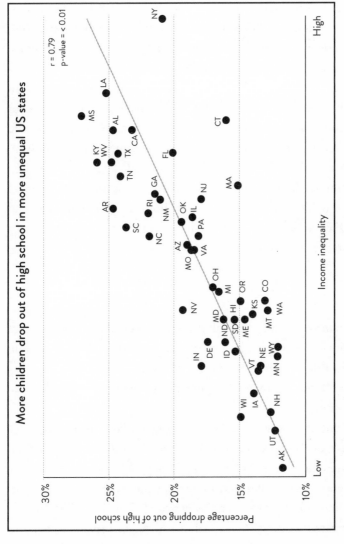

Figure 19. *Source:* Richard Wilkinson and Kate Pickett, *The Spirit Level: Why Greater Equality Makes Societies Stronger* (New York: Bloomsbury, 2010), 107, quoted in "The Spirit Level," The Equality Trust, accessed March 25, 2021, https://www.equalitytrust.org.uk/resources/the-spirit-level.

There are many things that adults do within high-performing schools that contribute to effective learning even in the face of massive social challenges. They can set a culture of high expectations, provide adequate support and coaching for teachers, and foster a culture of love and respect for students.

But the trend lines we see across rich countries and throughout the United States confirm for me what I have seen play out over two decades. Income inequality—and the many negative social factors that go along with such inequality—puts massive pressure on schools and teachers to ensure all students learn at their highest potential. Many things outside the four walls of a school affect academic achievement, such as steady housing, good nutrition, and safety. This pressure is often far too great for a single teacher or school to overcome on their own.

———

A reasonable takeaway from all the data shared above could be that inequality is a poor person's problem. If we reviewed the social and public health outcomes of the beneficiaries of income inequality (the top 50 percent or top 20 percent), we might assume they are doing just fine.

But one of the striking findings from Wilkinson and Pickett's review is that on many dimensions, inequality appears to damage all socioeconomic classes. "The truth is," they write, "the vast majority of the population is harmed by greater inequality."[14] This makes sense to me. It is hard to run a business well if you can't find enough well-educated workers. It is costly to invest in private security to protect your property from high crime activity. The COVID-19 pandemic has shown us how hard it is to stay healthy if you spend time in public spaces where people are sick. In short, it is better to be rich in an equal country than in an unequal one.

Michael Marmot, a British epidemiologist who wrote the much-discussed book *The Health Gap*, makes a different but related point. His research suggests that even in cases where the richest in a country are doing well, everyone else (the poor, the middle class, and even the upper-middle class) is worse off. It is a gradient. "All of us below the top have worse health than we would if we were at the top," he writes. "[In Britain], someone with middle income has eight fewer years of healthy life than if he were at the top."[15]

I can't help but wonder, What is the overall cost of all this inequality? How much wealth is stolen from us because so many of our youth are undereducated? How much productivity is lost because people are sicker or even dying younger than they otherwise would in a more equal country? How much entrepreneurialism and family stability are taken from us when we lock up and murder too many young men? What medical breakthrough, or technological innovation, or great work of art is locked up forever inside a young person whom we have undereducated, made sick, or allowed to die too early? These are perhaps the greatest costs of inequality.

—

I ask Father Clete Kiley, who has served as a priest in Chicago and a labor leader on a national level, about this relationship between public health and economic inequality. I am eager for his insight. Why does he think economic inequality and poor public health run together?

"Erroneous autonomy," he says.

I am a little confused. I ask what he means.

"Pope Pius XI in 1931 wrote a papal encyclical called *Quadragesimo Anno*," he explains. In it, he says that the root of "what has gone wrong in capitalism is this sense of erroneous autonomy. The idea that the market has to be free from any kind of intrusion. The individual has freedoms without any restrictions or responsibilities."

"But," he goes on, "there are times when the invisible hand of the market simply is destroying the common good."

"Where do you see this happening?" I ask.

"There are many examples. The whole Wall Street collapse in 2008. Businesses fighting [to discriminate against] gay workers. OSHA deregulation. Health issues like diabetes are high among low-income workers." He then turns to the COVID crisis, bemoaning how low-income and immigrant workers are being forced to work in meatpacking plants where COVID infections are running rampant. He points out how in Chicago, individuals from poor communities and communities of color are more likely to contract the virus.

"How did this happen?" he asks rhetorically. "It is erroneous autonomy gone wild." Communities can't be healthy when we ignore the ties that bind us. Our country can't be vibrant when our economy rips us apart.

# 7

# ECONOMIC INEQUALITY THREATENS OUR DEMOCRACY

The thing about democracy is that it requires all of us to be in it together. It simply won't work for long if we exclude big chunks of our community from the process. Our political history demonstrates this. We have survived existential threats to our country by enfranchising and empowering a broader base of people: Enslaved people. Women. Immigrants. Drawing new people in is how we have kept our democracy alive.

Our economy does not stand outside of our democracy. They are not twin silos standing independent of each other. They are vines that intertwine and lean on one another as they reach upward. A robust democracy needs an inclusive, vibrant economy to thrive. When our political system and our economic system draw people together toward a common identity and a shared future, they feed on and incline toward each other. When our democracy tries to bring people together while our economy tears them apart, the vines detach, and everything tumbles down. We can't simultaneously have a political system that brings us together and an economy that tears us apart.

Economic inequality threatens our democracy. People who do not believe their economy will serve everyone will rarely believe their political system will do so, and people who fail to believe in their political system won't participate in it. Democracy dies without participation.

Democracy is particularly sensitive to a unique form of inequality: the sense of *rising* inequality. Static inequality leads to disinvestment. But rising inequality—the sense that the rich are getting richer and the poor are getting poorer—leads to upheaval.

As we have seen, we do not face a static form of inequality that, unjustly or justly, has existed for some time without toppling the system. We live in an economy that continues to grow, but in which the gains are going nearly exclusively to the highest earners and the wealthiest.

This widening gap in inequality threatens our entire democracy. We see it play out most clearly in our decreased social mobility, our increased distrust of one another, and our relatively low levels of participation in the democratic process.

## Social Mobility

In America, we celebrate the stories of the entrepreneur who started with little and became rich by building a transformative empire. Andrew Carnegie was born in a one-room house in Scotland. John D. Rockefeller was one of six children of a lumberman who became a traveling salesman. Henry Ford came from a farm in southeastern Michigan. Even in our modern economy, we lift up the stories of those who built something out of almost nothing. Steve Jobs was the adopted son of blue-collar suburban Californians. Oprah Winfrey was born to an unmarried teen mother in Mississippi. Andy

Grove, cofounder and longtime head of Intel, was a Hungarian refugee who arrived in the United States at the age of twenty.

The story of social mobility is central to our American narrative. If all men are supposed to be created equal, then equality of opportunity (economic and political) must flow from that premise. Social mobility is proof of our egalitarianism. Contrast that with the rigid class structure of eighteenth-century England, where nobility remained nobility and the rest remained the rest. It is the possibility of social mobility—that no matter what family you were born into, you can achieve the highest status—that set us apart, demonstrating to ourselves and to the world that we are unique. We are a country that values innovation, hard work, and talent over pedigree and inherited social status. This is what has made us the strongest economic powerhouse in the world.

While many economic historians can debate how broadly true this story ever was, data suggests that social mobility is more dramatically limited today than in the past. In fact, we have become less socially mobile than almost any other Organisation for Economic Co-operation and Development (OECD) country. Americans are more socially fixed than we were a half century ago.

Miles Corak, an economics professor currently at the Graduate Center of the City University of New York, has looked at one dimension of social mobility, which he calls "intergenerational elasticity." He analyzes how much of one generation's income disparity will be mirrored by the next generation. If a country has an intergenerational elasticity of 1 (or 100 percent), all of the earning differential of the parents will be wholly passed along to their children. That society is completely fixed. If a country has an intergenerational elasticity of 0 (or 0 percent), none of the parents' earning differential will be passed along. That society is completely egalitarian, at least when it comes to inherited income advantage.

In Corak's analysis, the United States has an intergenerational elasticity of 0.47, which means that nearly 50 percent of the earnings differential between two adults will be passed along to their children. This is higher than almost any other OECD country. We are closer to China in our social mobility than we are to Canada, Australia, or Germany.[1]

When you look at social mobility in America over recent decades, you see some movement but not enough to suggest full equality of opportunity. Over half of all people in the bottom quintile of earnings remained there a decade later. More broadly speaking, over three-quarters of Americans who started in the bottom quintile didn't make it to the median earnings level within ten years.[2]

Just as we saw in the review of wage and wealth inequality, social mobility is negatively affected by other forms of marginalization, particularly race. For children born into households at the bottom income band, two-thirds of white Americans will move up to a higher one as adults, whereas fewer than half of Black Americans will do so. For those born into middle-income families, 56 percent of Black adults will fall to lower income bands as adults compared to only 32 percent of white Americans.[3]

Contrast this with the eras of great innovation and economic growth in the latter half of the nineteenth century. Our richest Americans today, those we hold up as examples, are more likely to come from backgrounds of relative privilege than they were a century ago, when people like Ford and Carnegie came from so little. Among the top ten richest Americans in 1918, four came from poor backgrounds and two more were the sons of small business owners.[4] Among the top ten richest Americans in 2020, most came from well-educated middle- or upper-income families. They were the children of lawyers, congresspeople, dentists, and professors.[5]

"Carnegie, Ford, they started with nothing," Jamaal Nelson tells me one afternoon. "But today, you've got to be born into wealth rather than work into wealth. If you're not born rich, you can't accumulate financial wealth for yourself and your family."

Wealth is becoming increasingly concentrated among the descendants of those who already had it. This class rigidity flies right in the face of the American ideal that those who pull themselves up by their bootstraps have a fair shot of making something of themselves no matter what station in life they were born into.

## Social Cohesion

On September 17, 2011, hundreds of protestors convened in Zuccotti Park in New York's Financial District to occupy Wall Street. In the years preceding, the US had experienced the largest financial crisis in nearly seventy-five years. Sparked by a financial industry that had dramatically overextended itself through risky mortgage lending, the impact on the US economy and on American households was dramatic. By the third quarter of 2009, nearly one million properties were being foreclosed on *per quarter*.[6] Over thirty million people lost their jobs[7] and "Americans saw [their] wealth plummet 40 percent."[8] Yet not a single high-profile person went to jail for their role in this financial crisis. The combination of rising inequality, massive economic hardship, and no public accountability for those who led the financial institutions that had caused the crisis led to a wave of rising anger.

As the Occupy Wall Street (OWS) movement grew, that anger was palpable. People carried signs that read "The Financial District is responsible for most of the poverty and suffering on this planet," "It's time the fat cats had a heart attack," and "Our Economy is Modeled on a Cancer."[9] As the protest in Zuccotti Park swelled, it was replicated across the country. By October of that year, more than a third of Americans supported the protest, with over half of Democrats supporting it.[10] OWS served as a critical predecessor to movements such as Black Lives Matter (BLM) and Bernie Sanders's unexpectedly popular 2016 presidential campaign.

The Zuccotti Park protest is long over, but the sentiments it tapped into were strong and still linger persistently. The framing of OWS, that the "99 percent" must rally to demand an end to dominance by the "1 percent," is still present in communities across America.

On an unseasonably warm Monday night in a recent December, I attended a rally outside the Chicago Board of Trade. Hundreds of people gathered to protest a tax bill that aimed to cut health insurance and social services for many Americans while giving tax breaks to the wealthy.

At this rally, I saw terrifying signs like "May the blood of the proletariat trickle down to the working class." I heard a preacher who worked on the University of Chicago campus rally the crowd to "shut shit down and burn shit down." I heard elected officials and even a major candidate for governor talk about the evils of the corporate class. Everyone agreed that corporate owners and managers cared nothing for everyday Americans. The protestors' job, they claimed, was to fight back. They must remind business leaders of the working class's collective power and the weakness of their own corporate class.

After decades of rising inequality, many Americans believe that their lives are less economically stable and their futures less optimistic. A sense of class-based injustice has boiled over into concentrated rage. For many, particularly those on the left, this anger is focused on the owners and managers of the businesses that maintain our financial systems. Large swaths of Americans do not believe that our financial sector, our businesses, and those that fuel our economic growth engines are in it for the common good. In fact, many believe these people are a threat to our country. As evidenced by the OWS signs, this anger is not abstract, but concrete and personal. When Senator Bernie Sanders speaks of the system being "rigged" against 99 percent of Americans, he targets blame at the "greed, fraud, dishonesty, and arrogance" of today's business leaders.[11] Senator Elizabeth Warren points to financial industry CEOs as those who "wrecked" the economy and "destroyed millions of jobs."[12] According to public opinion research by Gallup, by 2020, only 19 percent of Americans reported that they had significant confidence in "big business," down from a high of 34 percent in 1975. In fact, Americans had higher confidence in almost every other institution—including religion, the presidency, organized labor, the medical system, and the criminal justice system—than they did in big business. Sadly, the only institutions that Americans had less confidence in than big businesses were TV news, internet news, and Congress.[13]

For others, this anger is focused on the government. Only 18 percent of Americans in a 2017 Pew Research Center Poll reported that they trust the federal government to do the right thing "just about always" or "most of the time." This distrust is commonly shared among both political parties, with only 22 percent of Republicans and 15 percent of Democrats saying they trust the government "most of the time."[14] Notably, this survey showed that Americans' collective confidence in our government had declined over the previous two years: compared to the same poll in 2015, respondents felt the government was doing worse in almost every area surveyed, from helping people get out of poverty to ensuring access to health care.

For many people I talked to for this book, the 2008 financial crisis represented a pivotal moment in forming their view of how our government and our economy conspire to help out only a small number of people. Few people, though, remained as incensed by it as Jamaal, who had seen the tragic results firsthand in his hometown of New York City.

Over the years, Jamaal has come to the conclusion that the idea of a meritocracy in America is a myth—a myth that was shattered with the trillion-dollar bailout of the financial industry. As he sees it, for decades, the titans of industry preached the gospel of capitalism: work hard, take risks, and don't rely on government assistance to get by. When workers got laid off or communities were harmed by the closure of a plant, these titans would say the market was correcting itself, which was natural and to be expected.

But the moment the big banks got into trouble, they received a government bailout. Jamaal saw it as a "socialist strategy," plain and simple. But it was socialism for the rich and powerful, not the average working person. "These folks did nothing to earn that bailout." This moment uncovered the real beliefs our leaders hold about capitalism. The market is designed to protect owners and senior executives, and government policies support that imbalance. Myths of independence and autonomy and self-reliance are just that—myths. They are used to justify depriving most Americans a share in the massive bounty of economic growth. But they are thrown out the window as soon as the rich and powerful need help.

Arlie Russell Hochschild, in her powerful book *Strangers in Their Own Land*, illustrates this deep distrust of government from another vantage point. She uncovers a "deep story" that Americans living in and around Lake Charles, Louisiana, have developed. They see themselves as waiting in a line on a hill. At the top of the hill is the promise of the American dream: that hard work and playing by the rules will grant them, if not financial prosperity, then at least financial stability for themselves and for their children. They have been waiting in that line for a long time, but the line is not moving. In fact, they are beginning to perceive other people cutting in line—immigrants, welfare recipients, LGBTQ people, even land and animals protected by environmental regulations. And in their view, these "line cutters" have been ushered in by the federal government, and in particular by Barack Obama.

So the surest way to ensure they move forward in the line up the hill is to eliminate the role and power of the federal government. Regardless of what the federal government is trying to do to make the lives of everyday Americans better—from financial regulations that will prevent the next Great Recession, to broader access to health care for middle-class Americans, to environmental regulations that will make the water cleaner and the residents who drink it less sick—they distrust the federal government and are determined to scale it back.

As Hochschild's "deep story" points out, this anger is not just directed at a faceless government but infused with racial and classist undertones. The 2016 election brought much of this racial resentment to the forefront. Studies have noted that those who voted for Republican candidate Donald Trump that year were more motivated by "racial anxieties" than economic concerns.[15] A 2015 *Esquire /* NBC News survey found that Americans were getting angrier, but white Americans and Republicans were angriest.[16] Their ire was directed at immigrants, the financial system, and the political establishment.

While those on the right may direct more anger at the federal government and those on the left may direct more at big business, what both sides of the political aisle share is increased antipathy toward fellow citizens on the other side. The Pew Research Center has measured partisanship for over two decades, finding dramatic increases over that time. In 1994, at the height of the anti-Clinton House wave and the dawn of the "Contract with America," 21 percent of Republicans had a "very unfavorable" view of the

Democratic Party and 17 percent of Democrats had a "very unfavorable" view of the GOP. By 2016, those numbers had tripled (Figure 20).[17]

Even the language we use to describe one another has become fraught. The same Pew study found that 41 percent of Democrats and 45 percent of Republicans viewed the other party as "a threat to the nation's well-being." It is mind-boggling that nearly half of each party's base views the other party as an existential threat to our country.[18] Perhaps the most telling is that an earlier study found that roughly a quarter of those who describe themselves as "consistently liberal" or "consistently conservative" would be unhappy if a family member married outside the party.[19]

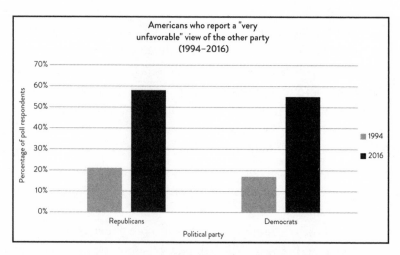

Figure 20. *Source:* "Partisanship and Political Animosity in 2016," Pew Research Center, June 22, 2016, https://www.pewresearch.org/politics/2016/06/22/partisanship-and-political-animosity-in-2016/.

This level of partisan suspicion merely mirrors the broader distrust that happens in unequal rich societies. In a review of data from the European and World Values survey, Richard Wilkinson and Kate Pickett find that more equal rich countries are three times more trusting than unequal rich societies. On the low end of the spectrum, in unequal countries like Singapore and Portugal, only 20 percent of residents say that most people can be trusted. On the high end, in Scandinavian countries, over 60 percent believe most people can be trusted (Figure 21).

The same findings play out across states in the US. People in the most equal states are almost three times more trusting of their fellow citizens than those in the most unequal states (Figure 22).

Trust serves as the basic bedrock upon which strong democracies are built. And by trust, I don't mean blind acquiescence to another's viewpoint or actions. Our Founding Fathers built a system of checks and balances—within the federal government's branches and between the states and the federal government—that acknowledged a productive level of wariness. But a baseline level of trust—in our institutions, our mutual legitimacy as citizens, in the workings of our civic engine—is required to participate in the public square and to accept the outcomes of the democratic process. Without such trust, people would opt out of the democratic process and not accept elections or legislation as legitimate. We see this play out consistently in autocratic regimes. So when only 25 percent of Americans believe that most people can be trusted, we see a threat to the workings of our democracy.

## Democratic Participation

Our social structures are ossifying. No matter how hard we work, the chances that we can improve our economic station dwindle. Many are sprinting just to stay in place. We look around to see who is to blame. CEOs. Government. Democrats. Republicans. Line cutters. The other side becomes a threat to our well-being. When they win,

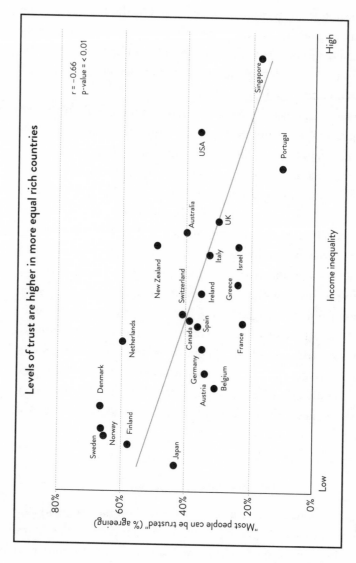

Figure 21. *Source:* Richard Wilkinson and Kate Pickett, *The Spirit Level: Why Greater Equality Makes Societies Stronger* (New York: Bloomsbury, 2010), 52, quoted in "The Spirit Level," The Equality Trust, accessed March 25, 2021, https://www.equalitytrust.org.uk/resources/the-spirit-level.

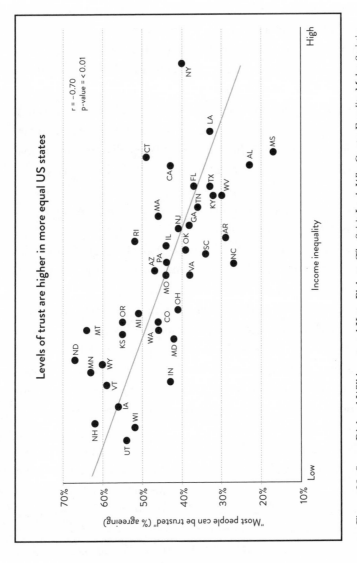

Figure 22. *Source:* Richard Wilkinson and Kate Pickett, *The Spirit Level: Why Greater Equality Makes Societies Stronger* (New York: Bloomsbury, 2010), 53, quoted in "The Spirit Level," The Equality Trust, accessed March 25, 2021, https://www.equalitytrust.org.uk/resources/the-spirit-level.

elections must be rigged. Perhaps the most damaging result of economic inequality is the resulting belief among wide swaths of our country that participation in democracy is futile.

This is why more unequal rich countries have lower civic engagement than more equal rich countries. Frederick Solt, a political scientist at the University of Iowa, has analyzed three types of civic engagement among developed countries.[20] He looked at people's view of *political efficacy*, measured by the degree to which survey respondents agreed with the statement "People like me don't have any say in what the government does." He looked at *interest in politics*, measured by survey responses to the question "To what extent would you say you are interested in politics?" Finally, he looked at *voter turnout* in national elections.

On all three dimensions, a country's income inequality was the greatest, or among the greatest, variable in predicting lower civic engagement. That is, citizens in unequal rich countries more often believe the government doesn't value their views, more frequently express a lack of interest in politics, and are less likely to vote in national elections. This could explain in part why the United States, which is one of the least economically equal developed countries, ranks thirtieth out of thirty-five OECD countries surveyed in terms of the percentage of the voting-age population who participates in elections.[21]

Mike Espinoza has seen firsthand how inequality depresses democratic participation. He remembers the brief period he spent organizing Latino voters as the Texas State director for Mi Familia Vota. Before the 2010 elections, Mike led a nonpartisan campaign to raise the number of Latino voters in key districts. On the East End of Houston, he worked in Mexican American communities where most had been born in the US. Like Mike's family, many of these community members could trace their lineage in this country back a number of generations. On the southwest side, he worked in communities with many more naturalized immigrants, who had arrived in America more recently.

What he saw was remarkable to him. "The naturalized immigrants voted at crazy high rates. But the native-born Latinos did not."

"Why?" I ask.

"Well, many of the [native-born Latinos] just didn't grow up feeling any sort of obligation. It wasn't like going to church. It wasn't like going to work."

He continues, "I think I boiled it down to, there was no pressing need in their life," explaining that people's basic attitude was, "I'm going to take off work so I can vote for what?" What had voting ever gotten them? How was their community better off because of leaders in office? At the end of the day, they weren't able to see any benefit in the cost-benefit analysis. The sacrifice to vote—to give up on work time and maybe lose wages and maybe have to defer some critical home or family care—just wasn't worth it.

———

Jamaal grew up in a home with both deep love for and deep skepticism about America. This ambivalence was framed by his father. Jamaal remembers the stories of his dad's childhood poverty—the outhouse, the stretches of hunger, the barely habitable home. His father would say, "It's only in America that I could have gone to the military, gotten a job, and been able to take care of my family. I have traveled the world in the military and there's no greater country than America."

"But she doesn't love Black people," he would add. "America is a great country, but it is not a fair country."

The experiences of millions of other Americans confirm this contradiction. There are too many people, Jamaal says, "who have never believed in equality, that they are an equal member of a democracy." That becomes all the more true when there is a widening gulf between the top 1 percent and everyone else. When people see their real wages stay the same, but their costs rise. When people are decimated by financial collapse, but the titans of industry get bailouts. It shatters what little faith they have in the story of America. As Jamaal puts it, "Economic injustice prevents you from even imagining the American Dream." Economic inequality threatens the very beliefs and behaviors that make our democracy work.

Even worse, it strikes at the core of who we are as a nation.

# 8

# ECONOMIC INEQUALITY ASSAULTS OUR VALUES

A video shows Ben Chin standing on a Lewiston street corner, wearing an orange fleece jacket over a blue-and-white-checkered shirt. He looks like a politician straight out of an L.L.Bean catalog, which I imagine works in Maine. His wife, Nicola, is wrapped in a sweater and vest and scarf, her belly obvious even beneath the layers. She is due to give birth to their first child in a week. There is a sad weariness in both their eyes. They are smiling, but Nicola's smile in particular is uncharacteristically fragile. Her lips quiver slightly at the edges. But her eyes are locked onto Ben, fiercely and warmly.

A few hours earlier on this Monday in October 2015, Ben's phone and email started blowing up. Overnight, posters had popped up throughout town urging residents, "Don't Vote for Ho Chi Chin." The poster's background was red with a hammer and sickle repeating across the top border. A caricature of an Asian face loomed large and menacing next to the admonition. This specter of the old "yellow peril" stereotype descended two weeks before the 2015 mayoral election in Lewiston, Maine's second-largest city.

"Next week, we are expecting to bring our first baby into the world," Ben tells the crowd, "and that child is going to have the same last name that was up on that sign today."

Pivoting to the central message of his campaign, Ben says, "As hard as this day has been for us, it is harder to live in a building that doesn't have heat. It is harder to work for twelve hours a day and go home tired, wanting to take a hot shower but you can't, because someone has denied you hot water. We are not going to back off an inch to build a city where every single child—no matter the shape of their eye, no matter their income—[can] grow up . . . having what every human being deserves."[1]

I was curious. What was it about Ben's inspiring and inclusive message that invoked such a vile reaction? Nicola is a friend of mine, so I asked her to introduce me to her husband. I wanted to learn from Ben directly what it was about Lewiston that made Ben's anonymous antagonist believe that appeals to racism would work to keep Ben from being elected mayor.

—

The story of what brought Ben to this campaign begins with his family, particularly with his paternal grandfather, the youngest child of a large family in a poor village in China.[2] His family couldn't afford to raise him, so they sent him to the United States alone, as an undocumented immigrant during the Great Depression. As a nine-year-old, his grandfather worked as a busboy in a New York Chinatown restaurant. He had "no family, no English, no money, no safety net, just nothing," Ben says. Because of a chance encounter one day, his elementary school principal took notice and brought him under her wing. With her support, he eventually graduated from high school.

He went on to serve in World War II, go to college, and start what would become a successful business. By the time Ben's father was born, his grandfather lived with his family "in one of the nicer parts of Manhattan." With his father's support, Ben's dad was able to earn his PhD in engineering at Syracuse University and become a professor.

Ben's mom, on the other hand, grew up in a different world. She was the white daughter of a white concrete block factory worker in Syracuse. "My grandpa was always changing his own oil and tinkering around with stuff," Ben shares. He remembers going out with his grandpa on a winter day when it was twenty below zero to help him unfreeze all the locks. "He had a sense that what makes life fun is you work your day job and you work around the house, and isn't that an awesome life?"

Ben's parents met, had two children, and divorced all within a couple of years. His mom moved with Ben and his sister in tow to Mt. Lebanon, a tony white suburb twenty minutes south of Pittsburgh, where she married a Presbyterian pastor. But even with all these changes, Ben remained close to his father.

As a result of this lineage, Ben admits he "grew up wicked patriotic"—not from his mom's side so much as his dad's. His grandfather held a deep reverence for the country that gave a poor undocumented child living alone a chance at a better life. Over time, Ben developed a "healthy skepticism" for the myths about America that didn't always ring true. But he adds, "I still retained a sense that there is this part of being American that is awesome and special and to be treasured."

Ben graduated from Mt. Lebanon High School in 2003 and went to Bates College in Lewiston, Maine. During his sophomore year, he became active in local community organizing. "The city administrator decided to put a road diagonally through downtown.

The chaplain's office [at Bates] was asked to send somebody [to a community meeting about the proposed road], so I went."

What he saw was "just so completely outrageous." A city official stood in front of a room stuffed with people going through a Power-Point presentation. The gist was that people in that room were going to lose their homes and it was a done deal. After the meeting, a representative of the Maine's People Alliance (MPA) jumped up on a table and shouted at the audience, "If you think what you heard tonight is bullshit, come to this meeting at 6:00 p.m. on Tuesday because we're going to talk about how to fight this."

Ben signed on. For the next two years, he volunteered with the MPA, which won the fight about the road. When he graduated, the organization had enough money to hire him on. He has been working there ever since.

Four years after Ben began working at the MPA, progressive Lewiston mayor Larry Gilbert had already served three consecutive terms, the limit, and so couldn't run again. Bob Macdonald, a proto–Donald Trump candidate, ran to replace him on a bombastic racist platform. He would go on to tell Lewiston's growing immigrant community to "leave [their] culture at the door"[3] and claimed that America was a land of "one culture, one language, and one set of values."[4]

Ben remembers everyone thinking, "this guy is never going to win." And for a time it looked like they were right. In a crowded field, Macdonald finished a distant second in the general election, squeaking into a subsequent runoff election. He seemed headed toward defeat. But his opponent in the runoff died four days before the election, so Macdonald edged out a win, earning only one hundred more votes than his dead opponent. Two years later, in 2013, Bob Macdonald's racism had become normalized, and he won reelection in a landslide.

By 2015, progressives, immigrants' rights activists, and working-class champions were desperate to beat this racist mayor, but no clear candidate was stepping up. The week after Christmas in 2014, Ben and Nico were driving through Scranton, Pennsylvania, on their way back from visiting family. At a roadside Mexican restaurant, they had a long conversation about whether Ben should run. "So we were just having chips and salsa and [were] like, 'You know what? This isn't necessarily what we thought, but let's go for it.'"

Ben, a thirty-year-old Asian American activist, was not the typical candidate for mayor in predominantly white working-class Lewiston, so he knew he would have to hit the ground early. In most years, "people take out their [candidacy] papers a couple of weeks before Labor Day and no campaigning starts until September. We launched in March."

Ben focused on getting to the doors and talking to the voters. From his work at the MPA, he knew housing justice was going to be at the core of his campaign. His time going door-to-door was spent eliciting people's stories, especially about housing.

And what he heard was heartbreaking. Some residents of Lewiston had their heat cut off in the dead of Maine's brutal winters. Others lived in housing with black mold or had bedbugs so bad, "some kids would be covered in bites the way someone would be covered with chicken pox." Landlords allowed pipes to burst and abandoned buildings to decay after taking months of rent.

Ben's campaign picked up steam, but so did the opposition. Housing may be inadequate in the downtown core of Lewiston, people admitted, but there were many causes. City administrators said they didn't have the budget to enforce the building codes. Some landlords claimed their business model didn't give them enough profit to invest in the buildings. Bob Macdonald and his compatriots put much of the blame on Lewiston's immigrant communities, faulting them for the downtown's destitution.

Heading into the home stretch, Ben's campaign shattered a state fundraising record.[5] His message was breaking through. He was succeeding at crafting a narrative for Lewiston grounded in shared values. "Lewiston may not be Maine's richest city, but we can be the city where every child grows up with a real shot at the American dream," he told voters.[6]

And then the posters came up. Fifteen days later, Ben lost the election by fewer than six hundred votes.[7]

———

Take a look at our flag: thirteen equal stripes and fifty equal stars, all together in a single bold fabric. I know of no other national flag that celebrates the bringing together of so many different parts into one moving symbol.

Our nation's flag is our nation's story. Each stripe reminds us of a disparate colony two and a half centuries ago joining into a common nation. Separated by almost 1,500 miles from the shores of Acadia to the Georgia swamps, these colonies covered a diversity of territory that equaled the distance from London to Gibraltar. Each star reminds us of every state that contributes to our common national identity, from the mountains of Wyoming to the plains of Nebraska, from the rivers of Louisiana to the beaches of Massachusetts. The central story of our flag is that no matter who we are or where we live in this country, we are bound together as equal parts in the fabric of our nation.

This is who we believe we are, or at least who we want to be. It is not perfect. Like many stories, our nation's mythology glosses over our most painful parts. Like many stories, it has sometimes been used to appeal to our worst instincts rather than our best selves. But it still remains our most powerful national symbol. It inspires us in our schools and in our paintings. It moves us when we see it at the head of the procession of our athletes at the Olympics. Even our national anthem is an ode to our flag.

But a flag that celebrates our coming together cannot fly with honor over a country whose economy is pulling us apart.

The story our flag tells—of unity across our differences—is embedded in our founding. A peek into our early history helps us understand how this story took shape.

Revolutionary Americans lived in a society described as a "cultural kaleidoscope."[8] While early settlers to the thirteen colonies were mostly English, by the early 1700s, immigrants were coming from many origin countries. Labor shortages in England caused the English government to restrict emigration. But the need for workers and the call for opportunity remained strong. Immigrants began pouring in from a broad base of other countries. By 1776, the majority of the Middle Colonies' population was not of English origin.[9] They were German, French, Swedish, Irish, Dutch, Scotch, Indigenous, and African (mostly enslaved). In the South, enslaved people from Africa outnumbered the people who claimed England as their cultural heritage.[10] There were few places in the world that had assembled a people from such a hodgepodge of national origins as the American colonies on the eve of the Revolution.

This immigration fluidity fueled a society that was much more culturally and economically egalitarian than those found in the home countries of European Americans' ancestors. Take a look at our Founders. John Adams was the son of a Puritan farmer who grew up in a four-room home his father built. Thomas Jefferson's father, by contrast, was a wealthy landowner who ensured his son began studying Latin, Greek, and French at age nine. Benjamin

Franklin was one of seventeen children born to a candlemaker. Alexander Hamilton was an orphan from the Caribbean. Our Founders lived in plantation economies and merchant economies, in rural outposts and in urban harbor cities. Some had families who had been in the New World for over a century, while others had only recently arrived. But they had a vision that brought them together. They imagined that these thirteen colonies, though stark in their differences, could come together as equal members of a new union grounded in the acknowledgment that "all men are created equal."

The budding country they lived in disbursed wealth among free citizens more broadly than America does today. Thanks to the herculean work of economists Peter Lindert and Jeffrey Williamson, we have a robust picture of how wealth and income were distributed in colonial America on the cusp of the revolution. Across all thirteen colonies in 1774, the top 1 percent of earners took home only 9 percent of the national income (remember, today the top 1 percent takes home over 20 percent).[11] When looking at the economies of New England and the Middle Colonies, incomes were much more equally distributed than they are in the US today.[12] Our Founders would likely be surprised by the amount of income and wealth now hoarded by the richest Americans.

Against this backdrop, *Common Sense* lit the colonies on fire. Its author, Thomas Paine, issued the pamphlet in January 1776, six months before the drafting of the Declaration of Independence. It served as a call to revolution among colonial Americans. Using simple prose and an accessible style, Paine sought to persuade the colonies that independence was just and that they had a moral calling to create a representative democracy.

*Common Sense* was massively successful, selling 150,000 copies—the equivalent of 12 million copies in a country our size today. Paine became a bard of the Revolution, articulating the values colonial Americans held dear. He inspired them to apply those values in the boldest way possible. Paine's work was so influential that it guided Thomas Jefferson in penning the Declaration of Independence.[13]

These same values inspired Paine to write *Agrarian Justice* twenty years later. In this work, he built on his previous demand for a more equitable government by calling for an economy that similarly worked better for everyday people. "Poverty," he wrote, is "created by . . . civilized life." Wealth is created by the use of cultivated land, he continues. This land, "the earth," is the "common property of the human race." Because of this equal and shared ownership in land, Paine proposed the creation of a "national fund" that would pay every person a set amount each year as compensation for the private use of property that was originally collectively owned. So the idea to pay every citizen for the right to use their shared wealth dates back over two centuries, to the Revolutionary era. A democracy that unites us all equally and an economy that acknowledges our equality—the philosopher of our revolution called for both.

But our Founders' views of "equality" were limited. Among the litany of tragedies that flow from the sin of slavery is that we were robbed of the wisdom of half a million enslaved people at the time of our founding. No reckoning of our nation's early values would be complete without incorporating slices of their insight. Still, I think we can say with certainty that the enslaved people who were forced to work without income so that others could amass wealth would have had strong views against economic inequality. Frederick Douglass, who had been born into slavery, certainly did.

Douglass was born on the eastern shore of Maryland around 1818. When he was twenty years old and living in Baltimore, he sneaked on board a northbound train, working his way to Massachusetts, and became free. For the next sixty years, he served as a national leader in abolition, equitable Reconstruction, and even international diplomacy.

Frederick Douglass's views on economic inequality are probably best captured in his 1856 editorial "The Accumulation of Wealth." Douglass had no problem with wealth, believing that it was the natural "condition of man" to acquire things "necessary for the security of life." Left unchecked, though, this bent toward "acquisitiveness" would prove ruinous. He looked out on the world of his time and saw that the "unlimited hoarding of wealth . . . has converted the entire civilized world into an abode of millionaires and beggars."[14]

Douglass concluded that a democracy and "an aristocracy of wealth" could not coexist. The growing inequality he saw expanding across the United States was a tool that would undo the liberties won by the Founders. Wealth's "accumulation in the hands of the few" had already led to "dreaded effects . . . of selfishness, devotion to private affairs, and a contempt of [the] public." The end result would be tyranny akin to what Napoleon III was unleashing in France at the time, enlisting the "sympathies of capital" to topple "personal liberty, freedom of speech, of thought, [and] of the press." To combat this chaos, he called upon "noble men" and "true statesmen" to "devise measures, which, while they will not hamper private enterprise shall yet prevent the undue accumulation of wealth in the hands of [few] individuals or associations."[15]

Douglass was not alone in viewing economic inequality as a threat to our burgeoning national values. In writing about his travels through early America, French diplomat Alexis de Tocqueville determined that the most important characteristic of our young country was the democratic nature of our "social condition." We had abandoned the European laws that passed down estates to a single heir in favor of "partible inheritance" that allowed all children to inherit property equally and prevented the amassing of "grand estates" across generations. He believed partible inheritance had an impact on our average wealth, as it disbursed wealth more quickly across generations.[16]

Tocqueville did not suggest that Americans were averse to wealth. In fact, he conceded that he "knew of no country . . . where the love of money has taken stronger hold on the affections of men."[17] But we valued work over inheritance, favoring a society in which people's labor and intellect carved out their lot in life rather than the privileges bestowed on them by birth.

I share this history not to paint the past in some utopian glaze but to give texture to our national story. We know our Founders did not live in an egalitarian paradise. It can be hard to reconcile that those who wrote "all men are created equal" also enslaved hundreds of thousands of people. It can be hard to trust their appeals to liberty and unalienable rights as they marched westward, displacing and murdering Indigenous peoples. As in our own lives, their actions often belied their beliefs.

While the story stands on shaky ground, it is still the story they have passed down to us. It is still our story. And that story—that people from different backgrounds could come together on equal footing to forge a shared future—was revolutionary.

When we move beyond our founding, we see that our country's history beats like a heart. We go through periods of pulling apart only to contract and come together once more. The stain of slavery and white supremacy nearly dissolved us, but the crucible of the Civil War pulled us together. The greed of the Gilded Age hastened us toward economic collapse, but the collective suffering and public works programs of the Great Depression bound us to one another once more.

In his final speech as president, Ronald Reagan quoted a letter he once received: "You can go to live in France, but you cannot become a Frenchman. You can go to live in Germany or Turkey or Japan, but you cannot become a German, a Turk, or a Japanese. But anyone, from any corner of the Earth, can come to live in America and become an American."[18] I think this captures this ethos of "togetherness across our differences" pretty darn well.

The data on today's economic inequality paint a gloomy picture in stark contrast to Reagan's optimistic vision. We see that as inequality grows, the fabric of our country is threatened. Poor social and health outcomes increase. Class structures ossify, limiting social mobility. Social cohesion begins to fray in dangerous ways, and people begin to check out of the democratic process. Inequality threatens any developed country. But for our country, built on the belief that we can come together across differences, rising inequality threatens the value that all Americans have an equal shot at "life, liberty, and pursuit of happiness." Inequality strikes right at the core of what it means to be American.

———

A landlord named Joe Dunne put the posters up in Lewiston. He wanted to protect his right to hoard wealth, and he knew the posters would have an impact. For much of the past century, Lewiston has been a town struggling with transition. It boomed as a textile mill town after the Civil War but declined after World War I, when milling became a less profitable enterprise because of stronger competition, changing fashions, and the rise of synthetic fabrics.[19] By 1970, the remaining three textile mills employed roughly 10 percent of the city's working population.[20]

All this economic change took a toll. As mills closed and government programs encouraged homeownership, people left downtown Lewiston. From 1970 to 2000, while America's population increased by 40 percent, Lewiston lost 15 percent of its residents.

Even today, Lewiston's poverty rate is twice that of the nation's. Nearly one out of every five Lewistonians lives in poverty. By 2014, the Lewiston area had one of the biggest "gaps between the rich and poor in the US."[21]

Racial and ethnic transitions have run parallel to these economic shifts. An influx of immigrants since 2000, led by Somali refugees, has stepped into the vacuum of downtown Lewiston. Between 2000 and 2010, the number of white residents of Lewiston decreased by almost 10 percent, while the number of Black residents increased nearly tenfold.

Joe Dunne's posters capitalized on the fear such social transformations had incited. What happened in Lewiston in the 2015 election was racism, pure and simple, but it's worthwhile to dig more deeply, unearthing the economic story that made such appeals resonate with some voters.

We have created—in Lewiston and across our country—an economy that rewards the income-hoarding, cost-cutting behavior of the Lewistonian landlord. We have allowed voids to form unchecked in previously thriving communities. We have held down the wages and wealth of most Americans while permitting the richest to thrive. People feel these injustices on a visceral level but aren't sure whom to blame. So when we throw the match of demographic changes onto the woodpile, the fires of nativism burn out of control. We have seen throughout this book that structural racism and economic inequality go hand in hand, challenging our deep national story that we are one nation out of many. When racism and economic inequality fuel each other in a vicious cycle, they strike at the core of our American values.

Like me, Ben doesn't have simplistic views about our failings as a country. "America was born in a tragedy of racism," he says. We were "a white settler movement that initiated multiple genocides on multiple Native peoples to claim a continent's worth of land, powered initially by slavery."

"But," Ben goes on, "I think within that tragedy that birthed the country, there was this rhetoric that could sow the seeds for the undoing [of these national sins]." In order to pull off this historic revolution, "people had to talk about freedom, and equality, and democracy. . . . For all the contradictions that are in America [at our founding], this idea of equality was real and alive" in a way it wasn't elsewhere in the world.

Our founding documents are not perfect. They were not handed to us on a mountain top, etched in stone. They were written by broken men in broken times and incorporated the racism and xenophobia and misogyny of their day. But as Ben points out, buried within these documents were the tools for us to become better than we were. These tools forged a nation whose existence was justified not by common tongue or homeland or church but by a shared commitment to our values and one another, no matter our differences. But as the Lewiston mayor's race shows us, an economy that pulls us apart cannot coexist with a democracy that requires us to stand together.

———

Inequality is not in and of itself bad, but left unchecked, it will stifle our collective potential to rise together.

"Inequality can sometimes spread growth," Angus Deaton writes, "if it shows a way for others to benefit from new opportunities. . . . Or inequality can become so severe, and the gains so concentrated in the hands of a few, that economic growth is choked off and the workings of the economy are compromised."[22]

We are facing income and wealth inequality at a level unseen in the modern era. It magnifies some of our worst inequalities, like those based on race and gender. It threatens our collective well-being. It limits our social mobility. It turns us on one another. It threatens our values.

There is no single solution that will address this breaking structure. We need a myriad of bold ideas, grounded in respect for our country and the many people who live in it, to begin to tackle this problem. So let's explore one possible remedy.

# A WAY BACK TOWARD ONE ANOTHER

# 9

# WHAT WE OWN TOGETHER

We know we face a degree of economic inequality that is unprecedented in modern times. We've learned how this inequality is linked to a litany of social harms. We understand that this inequality tears at our democracy and flies in the face of our national values. But what can be done about it?

To be honest, the solutions required to meaningfully address this complex problem are in turn complex. There is no single solution. There is no panacea, no painless remedy that once adopted will magically cure the ills we have allowed to fester over recent decades. We cannot, however, afford to be timid, afraid to apply new thinking. We must instead be bold and try out different solutions, even if they are imperfect. The alternative to this risk-taking is not the status quo; the alternative is that our society will become sicker. The civic fabric of our democracy will only unravel more quickly.

The solutions we consider should meet two criteria. First, they must have some impact on reversing or curtailing the speed of increasing inequality. Second, they must be in line with our national values.

The proposal laid out in this book—the Citizen Dividend—meets both criteria. But before we get to the meat of our proposal, we should first step back and acknowledge what we own as a society together. A just claim on wealth begins with accepting what is rightly ours in the first place. In our society, we have a clear sense of what types of things we own individually: our homes, our cars, our clothes. We have structures that make it clear what collectives of individuals own privately: corporations, business partnerships, social clubs. We even understand what the government owns on our behalf: land, the military, infrastructure, buildings. But we don't have a clear sense of what we own collectively by virtue of being citizens, as part of our participation and membership in our society.

Because of this lack of clarity, we tend to use these resources without consideration of their costs or benefits. We use them for our enjoyment, our peace of mind, our safety. Most importantly for this book, we use these collectively owned resources to create economic value. But because we have not been explicit about that economic value, we have not demanded that those who use our collectively owned resources to create wealth pay us back.

It's time for that to change.

---

For all the national buzz around the health-and-wellness company Asutra, I am surprised at how small its factory is. It sits on a modest lot next to an auto body shop, surrounded by bungalow-style homes in Chicago's Albany Park neighborhood. Only twelve people work in the company, in roles ranging from marketing to production. On an open floor, employees dressed in scrubs and hair caps and masks mix and make the products quietly. People are focused but not rushed. In the breakroom, there is a half-eaten cake and a "Happy Birthday" sign.

Stephanie Morimoto, Asutra's CEO, holds herself with a blend of warmth and regal confidence, as if your best friend from childhood became a working royal.[1] She is tall and thin, with short black hair she sometimes shaves on the sides. She is quick to laugh, willing to opine, and honest in her disagreements.

She describes the business of Asutra as "active self-care." Its products are all-natural and range from sleep support to pain relief to aromatherapy and skin care. "We want you to take care of yourself on purpose, so that you can take on anything," she says. I am most familiar with Asutra's products through my husband, who particularly loves the Mist Your Mood lavender and chamomile spray. He sprays our bedroom and his office in it. Sometimes, if I am being cranky, he just sprays it at me. Toby is not the only one who likes Asutra products. Nationwide, customers can find their merchandise in over four thousand stores like CVS, Kohl's, and Target. They have even attracted the attention of tennis star Venus Williams, who signed on as a part owner and spokesperson.

Asutra's reboot is relatively new. Stephanie purchased the company from its original owners in Houston in 2017. She has expanded it rapidly ever since. To understand why Stephanie became the CEO of Asutra and how she runs the company, you have to hear her talk about Connie Evans.

Stephanie grew up in Joliet, Illinois, the daughter of a doctor and a dentist and the granddaughter of survivors of the Japanese American internment camps of World War II. Despite the tragedy of internment, Stephanie's grandfather Paul taught her "this idea that even though you're jailed by your own government and your own country, you can't be bitter about it. You have to just deal with it and see the positive in life if you're going to succeed." Paul also taught her to "do what you love and everything else will follow." This charge lit a fire in Stephanie to be curious about finding her purpose in life and relentless in her drive to pursue that purpose.

Stephanie went from the public schools of Joliet to the Ivy League halls of Brown University. Upon graduation, she taught English for a year in Hiroshima (the town her great-grandfather emigrated from nearly a century before) and then spent two years doing strategy consulting for major national companies in Chicago. She left that work eager to dive into something more connected to her sense of purpose. A former colleague introduced her to the Women's Self-Employment Project, which Connie Evans had founded in 1986 to support Black women who were starting and growing their own businesses.

Connie believed that women were central to strong communities. She also knew that most people in this country are employed by small businesses. With these two foundational understandings, Connie concluded that when women-owned businesses were thriving, communities flourished. She therefore built an organization whose primary aim was to help women small business owners find their purpose and grow their companies. Similar to Paul's charge to Stephanie, the central questions Connie and the team at the Women's Self-Employment Project posed to their clients were "Who do you want to be, and how do you want to be in the world? What do you want to do in and with your community?" As Stephanie came to realize, "our job was to help [them] define and amplify that, and then do it."

Stephanie remembers a client in North Lawndale who was running a recidivism program, trying to help men coming back to the community from jail get jobs. It was nearly impossible. But rather than giving up, the client said, "Fuck it, I'm just going to build a company and employ them myself."

"This was when beehives became big," Stephanie explains. "She bought a bunch of beehives and put them on the roof of her building in North Lawndale. She built a company called Bee Love, which sells the honey and products, like soaps and shampoos, made from honey. They're still around. They sell at [the supermarket] Mariano's, local natural grocery stores, and at O'Hare and Midway airports." Supporting women-owned businesses like these was far more inspiring to Stephanie than consulting for the giant retail stores she'd worked with previously.

Stephanie loved working for Connie and the team. Almost everyone at the Women's Self-Employment Project was a Black woman. To learn from such impressive women of color was important to Stephanie. Among the many things Connie, in particular, taught her was "a better understanding of how systematic economic policy had kept Black and brown communities down."

She continues, "I didn't learn about it growing up or in school, but in addition to outright redlining, there [are] banking policies that won't serve African American and Latina women in Chicago. Connie was really good at teaching me this. She said, 'Look, these folks, banks won't serve them. The requirements aren't realistic for women who are of this income or asset level,' right? Yet that doesn't mean they shouldn't be able to save or not have to take payday loans.

"I learned a lot about the real policies in banking, housing, lending that I didn't know before, and then I realized, 'Oh, shit. This is so intentional.' This is so intentional, that we have purposefully cut whole swathes of people out of being able to access the capital and the services they need to build what they want."

It became clear to Stephanie—in a much bolder and more concrete way than ever before—how the social and economic ecosystem that surrounds a business accounts for much of its success. No matter how smart and hardworking business owners were, their path to financial success was hard if they were denied fair access to banking, were housed in a community with high crime, weren't educated in schools that taught them finance, or weren't raised with a personal network of influential people who could help eliminate barriers for them.

The flip side is also true. When business owners can launch with seed money from a bank or a family member, can hire well-educated and well-connected friends to work with them, and can house their business in a community that is safe and has high-quality city services, their chances of success go way up. As one writer quipped, successful "entrepreneurs don't have a special gene for risk—they come from families with money."[2]

But it's not just family money that comes into play. Public wealth also plays a huge role in business success. This includes the public education that business owners and their employees receive, the technology they use that was developed with government grants, and the energy grid built with public dollars that their businesses can plug into. All of those factors are significant in making sure a business can create value.

After a few years at the Women's Self-Employment Project, Stephanie moved with her now-husband, Matt, to New York. For the next fifteen years (in New York and San Francisco) she worked as a national leader at two nonprofits, helping scale and grow their work. But in 2015, when she and Matt moved back to Chicago, she wanted to start her own business. Leaning heavily on what Connie had taught her about the power of small businesses to invest in and uplift communities, she tells me how she "really wanted to create good jobs for people who needed them in Chicago."

Armed with insights from a wide-ranging career, Stephanie has built Asutra into a national brand in just a few years. And she has done so with the values and wisdom Connie Evans and so many others imparted to her. She's worked with employment placement firms to hire employees who are trying to reenter the workforce full-time. Of the people on her team, 77 percent identify as people of color, and 42 percent are Black. Employees earn a living wage. Benefits are available to all. The workplace is calm and respectful. Hours are scheduled in advance and respected.

And Asutra has become a success. In all of this, Stephanie sees the role and responsibility of business in community differently from many other CEOs. She has a deeper appreciation for all that goes into making a business successful, and it isn't just individual talent, hard work, and risk-taking. It takes a strong sense of purpose, a little bit of luck, and a big chunk of community wealth. In order to understand how an individual or a business can succeed financially, we have to acknowledge that it takes more than just chutzpah and private dollars. Every rich person and every profitable business uses wealth we all own together to create value. When we appreciate precisely what that public wealth is and how business leaders like Stephanie use it to turn a profit, it is clear why we deserve a Citizen Dividend. Building off the incredible work of Peter Barnes, I'll lay out that in modern societies, we own four types of resources collectively.

## Natural Resources

Our first collective assets are our natural resources: the soil from which we grow our food, the ground from which we mine our minerals, the rivers from which we harness power and transport goods, and even the sun and the wind, which increasingly provide us with power. These resources preceded the birth of our nation. They existed far before people settled on our continent. They were not created by us but are available for use by all of us. Peter Barnes calls them "the gifts of nature we inherit together."[3]

That does not mean that we do not assign ownership or use rights to these resources. Obviously, we do. Humans have a long history of giving land to individuals and to collectives. We allow individuals and corporations to own mines or to attain the rights to extract minerals from the ground. Rivers are often public-use thoroughfares. And while no one owns the sun or the wind, we do allow private ownership of the tools and land used to capture solar and wind energy and turn them into consumable power.

But assignable use and even private ownership cannot belie the fact that we merely permit exclusive use of resources that were created before us and without us. The land and the rivers and the sun and the wind existed in a natural state when we came upon them. Following in their centuries-old legal traditions, our European forebearers came together on this soil and decided to assign private ownership and permit restrictive use of these resources.

It's time to reclaim the idea that our natural resources belong to all of us. Thomas Paine writes, "It is a position not to be controverted that the earth, in its natural uncultivated state was, and ever would have continued to be, *the common property of the human race*."[4] Frederick Douglass asserted that "earth, air, fire, and water . . . should be free to all men, in virtue of their heaven-descended right."[5] While we may create legal frameworks that permit private use of these resources, we have not abandoned our collective ownership rights. Private use is a privilege granted by society.

## Societal Resources

In August 2011, Elizabeth Warren was running for US Senate in Massachusetts. At a campaign stop at Andover in someone's home, she delivered a now-famous speech:

> There is nobody in this country who got rich on his own. . . . You built a factory out there? Good for you. But I want to be clear. You moved your goods to market on the roads the rest of us paid for. You hired workers the rest of us paid to educate. You were safe in your factory because of police forces and fire forces that the rest of us paid for.[6]

These few simple sentences became the centerpiece of her progressive worldview, which so many have rallied behind. What Warren points to is another form of co-owned wealth: what I will call *societal resources*. These are resources that we all own in equal measure because they were paid for through our collective means for our collective use. In other words, these are what we pay taxes for. Societal resources are the infrastructure we build, the public safety we maintain, the basic education we provide every resident, and the energy grid we subsidize. We all own those societal resources equally.

Admittedly, some may pay more to build or maintain these resources because we have a progressive taxation system in America. But paying more or less for them in any given year does not give us more or less an ownership stake in them. From the moment we are born, even before we begin to produce value for society, we are granted the right to use these resources. Even if we lose our jobs or our personal wealth ceases to create value, we still retain the basic right to be safe, to move on roads, and to interact with literate educated residents.

## Inherited Systems

Prior generations created and passed down to us these societal resources we use every day. But they have also given us so much more. Over more than two centuries, our forebearers have built up complex social arrangements and systems that keep our society working. This is an even richer inheritance.

The most fundamental of these inherited systems are our Constitution and resulting federal system. They provide the legal framework for the workings of our government. But beyond this primary system, our forefathers and foremothers created a slew of other systems that enable us to create value in our society. Our intellectual property system incentivizes and protects innovations. Our judicial system and our courts give us peaceful redress for wrongs. Our financial systems—the markets and exchanges—enable us to readily invest in and collect returns in value creation.

We inherit these systems and the right to use them from our predecessors. They are the foundation we need to create and protect value. Some of these systems were created privately, like financial markets and exchanges. Most were created publicly: the judicial system, our governments, our patent system. But all of these systems are equally open to all of us. The idea is that no citizen gets to use more or less of our Constitution than any other. No American has an individual ownership interest in our courts.

Imagine a company like Ford or even Amazon. They were created in a relatively stable and peaceful society. Their intellectual property was protected through a preexisting system that was readily accessible. As these companies grew, they had access to courts to litigate disagreements. They were able to infuse capital in their strategic growth through ready access to financial markets.

Our ancestors created these systems for our collective use. When we use them as private actors, we are able to create value with much less friction than we would have without them. Without these systems, hardly anyone would be able to create value at all.

## Our Joint Participation in the Social Contract

The most abstract, but arguably the most essential, form of co-owned wealth is our collective agreement to abide by the norms and structures of society. We agree there is a notion of private property that deserves to be protected by the state. We consent to be governed by institutions. We accept that courts are places where we resolve significant private disagreements. We even all agree that coins and green paper currency have value that can be exchanged for goods and services.

No one alive served as the architect of this complex social contract. We have inherited this contract equally from our ancestors. We participate in it willingly. We punish infractions against these agreements. Because this contract runs so deep and goes back so long, we are hardly aware it exists. Much like how the air we breathe is fundamental to our biological existence, this contract is so fundamental to our social existence that we often do not see our tacit acceptance of it.

Many times, the social contract takes shape in the form of laws. When we steal from someone, we are punished. When we renege on a contract, we have to make the other party whole. But often the rules of the social contract are not written down. There is no law I know of that requires everyone to use the US dollar when buying something in this country. But when we go to a grocery store, we don't attempt to negotiate with the checkout person to pay for our food by exchanging used books we don't want anymore. We don't have a national curriculum in our country, but when someone has a high school degree, we assume they have a basic skill set in reading, writing, and math. Our laws do not forbid us from partnering with untrustworthy people, but when someone in our line of work is regularly known to break promises, we avoid doing business with them.

Without the social contract, we could not create much value at all. Imagine a country without a common currency or without a shared belief in private property. The fact that almost everyone wakes up every day and agrees to abide by our social norms and laws enables society to function. It is so natural to us that we mostly don't realize we are doing it. But it is still incredibly valuable. If people didn't do this, we could not as easily build factories, hire workers, or invent forward-thinking technologies. Every person who creates value in the modern world uses the social contract to help create that value.

———

I ask Stephanie to talk to me about how her views on businesses have changed since she started running her own small business. She pauses to think. "I don't know if anything has changed, but I have deepened some of my convictions."

"Like what?" I ask.

First, she talks about how businesses should be structured to serve a broader set of stakeholders, not just shareholders. "Why do we put profit above all else? What drives that?" she starts. She concedes that she knows it is because companies are owned by shareholders and run by executives with compensation tied to stock options, so shareholder profit drives all the major decisions. But, she asks, why don't more companies see giving "more ownership and profits to all the company's workers" as a central part of their success? Even her libertarian father-in-law, who grows his own food and hunts and even has a well on his property so he can avoid using public water, thinks it's "pretty abominable that today companies don't take care of their employees more."

"Today, we put shareholder value first instead of value for the employees or even the companies," she says. It doesn't necessarily have to be that way.

Second, she continues, companies bear a responsibility to society that too many are avoiding. "Elizabeth Warren makes this argument, that corporations get a lot of subsidy and support from the federal government," yet they avoid paying taxes. "Companies like GE can literally avoid billions of taxes."

In reflecting on what has made Asutra so successful so early, she points to a number of things, but in the end, she knows it is more than her hard work. So much of it has to do with luck. "You have to put yourself in positions to benefit from luck," she concedes, "but luck is a lot of it."

But luck isn't the only factor that enables business success. "We've just become an increasingly individualistic society that likes to believe that each of us made it where we are on our own merits and our own merits alone, when in fact, whether it's the Constitution or the financial system, or our families or the people that came before us and blazed different trails, we didn't get here on our own and just because we're talented."

Asutra is successful but, to paraphrase Elizabeth Warren, it didn't become successful on its own. It built upon the incredible wealth of our country to grow into a vibrant company. Stephanie acknowledges, "We have to ship goods and materials from various countries and states to where we are, so that's certainly one [form of public wealth we use]. We use the financial system. We took a loan to purchase the business, and that loan is backed by the SBA [the federal Small Business Association] and funded by taxpayers. We couldn't do what we do without the intellectual capital and skills that our employees and partners" have gained through the educational system. As a country, we have pumped an incredible amount of wealth into Asutra. Stephanie and her team have used that wealth wisely to create even more value.

Near the end of one of our conversations one day, I ask Stephanie, "As a business owner, do you worry about the impact of all this rising inequality?"

"Absolutely," she shares. "It is not stable for a democratic society to have this much inequality for this long." She knows businesses can't thrive if the fabric of society is fraying around them.

If we own our natural resources, our societal resources, our inherited systems, and our viable social contract equally and collectively, what are the implications in a capitalist society?

Simple. When an asset, owned by others, is used to create value, the owners of that asset have an enforceable right to a part of that value. As such, when businesses use our natural resources, our societal resources, our inherited systems, and our social contract to create profit, they owe a portion of that profit to the owners of those assets: us.

# 10

# THE CITIZEN DIVIDEND

For centuries, businesses have been issuing dividends to their share-holders. The concept is simple. When a company needs money to grow (say, to build a factory or invest in research or open new stores), it can collect this money from the general public. People give the company money, and in return, the company issues them stock, or a piece of ownership in the business. Because these investors now own a share in the business, we call them shareholders. When the company makes money, it can decide to invest that profit back into the business or return some of that profit to its shareholders. This payment back to shareholders is called a dividend. When shareholders sell their stock, buyers have the same right to collect that dividend payment in the future.

In 1980, Apple raised roughly $100 million from investors by selling shares to the public for the first time.[1] This original $100 million influx of cash allowed Apple executives to invest mightily in the future of the company. By 2020, Apple had become the twelfth-largest company in the world.[2] In July 2020, it announced that it would be paying out a dividend of $0.82 per share to anyone who held shares at that time, part of an effort that returned $22 billion to shareholders that quarter.[3] In years when a company is really successful and its profits are substantial, like Apple's, it can issue larger dividends than in years when it has smaller profits. But either way, big or small, shareholders have a claim to a slice of these profits because the money the original shareholders gave the business is part of the reason it could turn a profit today.

The concept of a Citizen Dividend is similarly simple. Because businesses use our wealth to create value, they should pay us back. Every year, businesses should return a percentage of their profits to citizens as payment for using our co-owned wealth to create those profits. If they use our wealth to create value, part of that value is ours.

While the concept is simple, the implementation is more complex. We should take time to flesh out these important details. To make it work, we need a broad coalition. We need workers' rights activists and champions of corporate social responsibility. We need economists and politicians. We need business leaders and voters. We need everyone who believes in the American value of "out of many, one."

If I flesh out a proposal with too many specifics, potential coalition members who agree with the broader idea may peel off because they disagree with a minor detail. I have also seen how crafty political leaders use details to beat back change. They claim to be in support of a new idea—and thereby burnish their credentials as change agents—but oppose the way the idea is implemented, thereby placating the powerful and preserving the status quo. In short, a proposal with too many details could die the death of a thousand paper cuts before it has had the chance to really live.

But I also know that an idea without some specifics is hard to rally around. We all need some details to give shape to new ideas. They help us make sense of the abstract and believe in the possibility of new things coming to life.

I'm going to thread this needle.

In this chapter, I'll give enough specificity to allow us to imagine the possibility, but not so much that it prevents us from building a broad coalition. There are many ways we could build out the Citizen Dividend. I hope academics, political leaders, workers, and business leaders will join me in this work to hammer out the details. Right now though, I want to focus on seven principles I think should define the Citizen Dividend. Whatever shape we give it in the end, the result should embody these basic principles.

### 1. A Simple and Common Definition of Profit

The business fundamentals of grocery store chains, airlines, banks, and hardware stores are all different. The realities of corporations and limited liability corporations (LLCs) and partnerships are similarly different. While we could try to come up with a different definition of profit for each industry and for each business structure that addresses their particularities, we would become mired in a complex web of specifics and exceptions. The system would be hard to understand, costly to administer, and vulnerable to special-interest lobbying.

A simple system is easier to rally people behind and easier to get off the ground. Therefore, we should use a common definition of profit across all businesses.

How we define profit is a major decision. Does it come before or after payouts to shareholders? Does it account for prior years' losses? Does it consider depreciation? There are countless other questions with meaningful considerations. How we define profit will have large implications on the amount available for Citizen Dividend payments.

One place to start would be to define profit as the net income businesses already report to the IRS each year. There are benefits to this: simplicity and commonality across all businesses. Every business has to file a tax return. There are also significant draw-backs, the biggest being that it conflates the Citizen Dividend with a tax. The Citizen Dividend is not a tax—as I'll discuss later—and setting the profit base as taxable business income risks riling up the antitax, antigovernment flank. It also intertwines the complex incentives we created in our nation's tax system with those that we have in the Citizen Dividend.

But establishing a major new dividend program for ten million American businesses is complex enough. Taxable business net income is already measured and reported. It seems to be the most prudent way to define profit.

## 2. A Simple Percentage of Profits That Makes for a Meaningful Dividend

There is no magic number that makes the Citizen Dividend work. On one end, it should be large enough that the dividend proves meaningful to people. They should have a real sense that the dividend can have an impact on their lives. Alternatively, it should not be so high that it stymies business growth.

Initially, we won't know the optimal rate for the Citizen Dividend. Nearly a century ago, the architects of the Social Security system couldn't anticipate what the ideal amounts of investment and payout would be. But in the words of Peter Barnes, it is important to "build the pipes first; then add water."[4] In 1940, the first payment on a Social Security claim was made. Ida May Fuller from Vermont received check number 00-000-001 for $22.54 on January 31, 1940.[5] In 2020, the average monthly Social Security payment was $1,513, and that excludes other social benefits, such as Medicare, that we've added since Ida May's time.[6]

I begin with a proposal that we should distribute 5 percent of business profits annually as a dividend. In 2015, US businesses (excluding sole proprietors) reported over $3.6 trillion in net income to the IRS. Of that income, 5 percent divided across 320 million Americans that year would have meant just over $570 per person or over $2,200 for a family of four.[7] This would have a meaningful impact on the lives of many Americans. The median household in America would see a nearly 3 percent boost in their income.[8] At the same time, it would leave the bulk of pretax profits for companies to use for their private purposes. From 2003 to 2014, the largest corporations in America paid back 91 percent of their earnings to their private shareholders without much outcry about how they were failing to invest enough of their profits back into the business.[9] In light of this, I doubt paying 5 percent of their net income to the public would stymie company growth.

Over time, though, we can change this percentage if need be. If 5 percent is too low for most Americans to feel an impact, we can tweak it upward. If it is too high for businesses to disburse the dividend and still invest in future growth, we can adapt it downward. But the point is to start at a meaningful yet modest level. Once we learn more about the impact, we can adjust.

### 3. No Loopholes

In our nation's tax structure, the government rewards certain behaviors with tax loopholes. Many of us know that the government gives tax breaks to individuals when we donate to charity, own a home, adopt a child, or go to college. Our government wants to encourage these activities that benefit the whole of society. Similarly, the government wants businesses to make charitable contributions, invest in the long term, and fully fund employee benefits and pension sharing programs. To encourage companies to engage in these activities, the government treats them favorably within the tax system. When businesses do more good, they pay fewer taxes. While specific tax loopholes can be debated on their merits, there is value in having a system that encourages businesses to engage in an activity the government finds positive.

But as we will see, the Citizen Dividend is not a tax. Therefore, the government must not be allowed to create exceptions to the distribution of the Citizen Dividend to reward behavior it values. The dividend is a return of value to the owners of whatever wealth was used to create that value. Should the government want to incentivize various actions among businesses, it can readily do so with the tax code. But the dividend is not designed to be the provenance of government tinkering to achieve those outcomes.

## 4. Real Distribution

Each citizen must receive an actual dividend in the form of cash in their pocket. It cannot be deducted from taxes or other payments owed to the government. In order for the full benefits of the Citizen Dividend to be realized—in order for citizens to feel like they have a stake in the growing economy and success of American businesses and one another—they have to receive the contribution directly. If the dividend becomes an abstract concept like a tax credit, the benefits will similarly become abstract.

By receiving an actual payment—a check in the mail, or a direct deposit in their bank account—each citizen will know that they have received something of real worth. It is this knowledge that the dividend is concrete and valuable that will drive many of the benefits.

## 5. Universally Applied

Every business must bear the responsibility of paying the Citizen Dividend. Partnerships, financial firms, hedge funds, pass-throughs—all of these receive differential treatment in our legal and tax codes. But to fulfill the purpose of the Citizen Dividend, any business that creates profit in a given year must pay part of that profit back to American citizens. Since the dividend is merely a return of value to those of us who co-own the wealth that was used to create that value, no type of business should be exempt. This means we should treat small businesses and large businesses similarly. If a business only turns a profit of a dollar, then it must return five cents to us citizens.

The only real exception to this principle should be to exempt sole proprietorships from the Citizen Dividend requirement. These are simple businesses whose owners have not gone through the steps required to establish a formal structure. They do not get the legal benefits we afford corporations, LLCs, and other business entities. These are frequently small businesses with few employees. Often, they are one-person shops. They are landscapers, tutors, graphic designers, web developers, housekeepers, and so on. The income a sole proprietor earns looks much more like labor income than business income. Since we do not subject labor income to traditional dividends, we should not subject sole proprietor profits to the Citizen Dividend.

Furthermore, if we were to require sole proprietors to pay the Citizen Dividend, the benefit would be low and the administrative burden would likely be high. In 2015, there were over 25 million sole proprietors in the US, reporting on average only $15,000 in net income. If we collected 5 percent of their net income for the Citizen Dividend, we would only collect around $770 per sole proprietor. Collecting $770 apiece from 25 million people seems like a heavy and expensive undertaking that would only barely increase each American's Citizen Dividend payment. It may not be worth the paperwork and human hours required to collect and redistribute the dividend from sole proprietors. It may be simply more efficient to focus on the fewer than ten million returns from corporations and other more complex businesses.

Some may fear that exempting sole proprietors from this payment may drive larger businesses to reclassify themselves as sole proprietorships to get out of issuing the Citizen Dividend payment. I don't think this is very likely. Sole proprietors assume full personal legal and financial risk for their businesses. When a sole proprietor gets sued or goes bankrupt, their personal assets—their home, their car, and the money in their bank account—can all be seized. More complex businesses, particularly those with multiple owners, are unlikely to expose themselves to that level of personal risk to avoid paying a small percentage of their profits.

With the exception of sole proprietors, every other business that uses our wealth to turn a profit must pay a dividend.


## 6. Universally Distributed

I have worked for years in and around low-income communities. I believe deeply that we must deliver more benefits to people who need more. In education, for example, we know that low-income students, special education students, and children who are just learning English often need more support. Making sure students have what they need to be successful has a greater impact than simply giving an identical service to everyone. This is also true of other social benefits. We should give more housing assistance to those who are homeless, more food to those who are hungry, and more health care to those who are sick. Our society is better when we give more to those who need more.

But the Citizen Dividend is different in that it recognizes that we all own wealth together. No one person—regardless of wealth or status—owns more or less of our co-owned resources than another. That is why the Citizen Dividend must be split equally among all of us, regardless of age, need, or preexisting wealth. At the same time, we should *also* have a government system that gives more benefits to those who need them most. But the Citizen Dividend is not a benefit program. It is a right of ownership. And we shouldn't conflate the two.

There are also practical reasons universality makes more sense. First, it makes it easier to administer. We don't have to work with a complex tax system to determine, calculate, and verify personal income for every American. We don't have to conduct audits, monitor compliance, or investigate and pursue fraud. When we take away the need to administer the dividend differently based on individual circumstances, the distribution becomes cheaper and easier.

Second, it is easier to convince Americans to implement a new benefit if it is universal. As Peter Barnes explains in his argument for a natural resource dividend, universality avoids the toxic language of winners and losers, of makers and takers.[10] Since there are no individual "losers" in the traditional economic sense—everyone gains a distribution—it is more likely to be accepted.

But furthermore, the perception of others claiming an "unearned benefit" is a powerful limit to social programs in America. Sarah Kliff, one of the best health care reporters in America, traveled to eastern Kentucky a few weeks after Donald Trump won the presidential election in 2016. This was a region of the country that best captured the paradox that the very places where so many people relied on Obamacare also voted overwhelmingly for a man who vowed to repeal it. Her reporting uncovered complex answers. Key to understanding this contradiction is recognizing the power of resentment for others receiving an unearned benefit. Many low- to middle-income Americans Kliff interviewed believed they were getting expensive but lousy insurance while poor Americans who opted not to work were getting quality Medicaid. One woman explained to Kliff that while she avoided going to the doctor because her deductible was too high, the unemployed around her "can go to the emergency room for a headache."[11] In the end, this woman's belief that less deserving people got a better benefit was one of the most powerful driving forces behind her willingness to back candidates who would take away her own health insurance. A dividend is less likely to be implemented if people feel others—especially "undeserving" others—are getting a better deal.

A final reason universality works is that it is harder to eliminate once implemented. As Barnes points out, Social Security is nearly impossible to take away, in part because people feel they have paid into the system. Most people expect to collect a Social Security check at some point in their life. Since most Americans have a sense of ownership in the Social Security system and they expect to personally benefit from it, it is difficult to get rid of. Similarly, with the Citizen Dividend, we are all owners and all beneficiaries. By allowing our co-owned wealth to be used, we have all contributed in some way to value creation. But perhaps more importantly, everyone collects a Citizen Dividend check every year. The distribution of that dividend will be hard for future governments to cut back.

## 7. Independence from the Government

Once we determine what the dividend will be and how to distribute it, we have to figure out who should run the program. Again, there are many thoughtful ways we can set the system up. But most importantly, it must exist separately from government. Undoubtedly, it should have the power of government enforcement behind it. But it should be independent of current institutions (e.g., the IRS, the treasury, and individual states' departments of revenue), and it should sit outside regular administrative structures (e.g., direct presidential or gubernatorial oversight). This does not mean that government actors can't have a role in determining how the system is administered. Perhaps the Citizen Dividend is run by an independent agency whose board is appointed by elected officials, something like the Federal Reserve. But its actors cannot serve at the pleasure of elected officials.

In a similar vein, the administrative costs to implement the collection and distribution of the dividend should come from the pool of profits being distributed, not from legislative appropriations. The dividend's distribution should not be held at the mercy of elected officials to adequately fund (or threaten to defund).

The Citizen Dividend is not a government program or a tax. It is a return of value to co-owners of wealth. As such, while it must have the enforcement of government behind it, it must exist separately from government.

—

Establishing a new payment to every American every year will be a bold undertaking. There will be many key decisions to make. We need the input of stakeholders and experts from throughout the country to do this right. Admittedly, it won't be perfect at the outset. It will require some tweaking and reforming along the way. But if we adhere to the seven principles outlined here, we maximize the chance of the Citizen Dividend's success.

And the Citizen Dividend's success will make our country stronger.

# 11

# THE BENEFITS OF A CITIZEN DIVIDEND

An annual distribution of over $500 per citizen from business prof-
its may seem modest. But if we make these payments year after
year, even $500 can begin to have a meaningful impact on both our
economy and our society. In this chapter, we'll look at the five main
ways that a Citizen Dividend benefits our country.

## It Chips Away at Economic Inequality

We won't remedy decades of rising inequality with a few hundred
dollars a year. But we have seen how most American families are
experiencing the "great squeeze," in which basic living expenses
are rising while real wages remain mostly flat. Raising the median
household income by 3 percent won't close the massive gap between
the average worker and the highest income earners. But it is a start.
It will help families in important ways. Most Americans would feel
the benefit of a $570 payment. A family of four would get $2,280,
which would cover the median rent for such a household for two
months.[1] It could pay for more than two months of an average

family's groceries[2] or almost two months of childcare costs.[3] Most American families don't have enough savings to absorb an unexpected $1,000 expense, so a Citizen Dividend could help them respond to a crisis.[4]

Jamaal has seen this firsthand. When I FaceTime him, the COVID-19 pandemic has prompted his family to escape crowded New York City to stay up in Rockland County with his mother. Despite the upending of his family's life, he appears full of equanimity. This is how I have come to know Jamaal in times of work crisis, and it is calming to see it now.

I ask him what he thinks the impact of $2,000 annually for a family of four might be. "Transformative," he declares. "It could help many of the families that I'm in deep relationships with meet some basic needs. Like kids' clothes or education or transportation."

He adds that the benefit is also emotional, in that financial security reduces trauma. "There is always the associated psychological stress of scarcity." I remember him describing this stress in his family when he was young as like the presence of an unwanted guest always living in your home. Even in expensive places like New York City and its surroundings, Jamaal acknowledges, "$2,000 would be really powerful. That's a month's rent or just some savings."

When I put the same question to Mike Espinoza, living in central California, he agrees. "Oh my gosh, $2,000 for a family of four? That's like a few months' rent [in Fresno]. That's a nice trip to restaurants and groceries and essential needs met." Recently, during the depths of the COVID-19 crisis, Mike worked with local funders to give out $500 to families most acutely affected. "Even $500 made a world of difference to the folks that really need it. It was a car payment, food, rent. It was meeting basic needs."

For someone like Bill Gates, $500 a year would not be a drop in the bucket. A family like the Waltons, who own Walmart, would not even notice $2,000 a year. But for many Americans—Americans who are working hard and seeing their basic costs rise faster than their wages—$2,000 a year for a family would meaningfully chip away at some of the stress of meeting basic needs. When most American families can't even withstand a $1,000 emergency, $2,000 goes a long way. It would help alleviate the pressures of the great squeeze. It would give families just a little bit of financial breathing room.

## It Limits the Shocks of Economic Disruption

With the onslaught of technological innovation and increased globalization, change crashes at a breakneck speed through our economy. Factories close in one part of the world, only to reopen elsewhere. Stores shutter in our neighborhoods as online retailers increase their market share. Jobs become obsolete as new technologies require automated production or upgraded skills.

We want many of these improvements to take hold. We want our economy to become more efficient, producing more goods at a lower cost. We want quality goods to be available to more people. But the cost of such accelerated change can be devastating. Many of us see the benefits of these changes in some way, but their costs are often borne by only a few of us. Moving an automobile factory out of Ohio to Central America may reduce the amount each of us spends on a new car by a few hundred dollars, but it decimates the Ohio town that housed the factory in the first place. Increasing online sales may reduce the cost of a hammer by a few cents, but it can upend the local hardware store.

Those who support our economic progress often fail to meaningfully respond to this pattern of distributed benefits but concentrated pain. Larry Summers, the US treasury secretary under President

Clinton, once compared opponents of factory closings to the "Luddites who took axes to machinery early in England's industrial revolution."[5] At best, when proponents of rapid economic change ignore the pains such changes can cause, they are being deaf to real harms in our country. At worst, like Larry Summers, they blame those who suffer as being lazy, undereducated, or insufficiently resilient to adapt to change.

I am not saying that the benefits of these advancements aren't real. Having access to cheaper, higher-quality goods is a boon for all of us. But not acknowledging the pain of these shifts ignores very real friction in rapid economic change. The result of this denial can be massive resistance to some components of economic advancement. In recent elections, we have seen large segments of the country rise up in resistance to economic threats they view as foreign (e.g., offshoring, free trade, immigration). Increasingly, even homegrown industries like Silicon Valley are drawing the ire of the public. In recent years, the percentage of Americans who say technology companies have a negative effect on our country nearly doubled, growing from 17 percent in 2015 to 33 percent in 2019.[6]

A Citizen Dividend begins to align better the benefits and costs of economic change. In our current economy, when a factory moves out of the country to take advantage of cheaper labor, the factory owners become richer but the American factory workers are out of a job. With a Citizen Dividend, if adapting to shifting economic realities really does increase an industry's profits, then every American will claim a percentage of those increased profits. Everyone gets a little more money in their pocket, not just the owners. Admittedly, a household receiving just over $2,000 won't offset the loss of a breadwinner's job. But it helps on the margins. And more importantly, if everyone benefits a little from major economic transformations, then opposition to these changes dampens a bit.

A meaningful Citizen Dividend reduces the friction of economic change.

Finally, a Citizen Dividend might block the most egregious and harmful disruptions. If proponents of rapid changes begin to get squeamish when they have to share the increased profits, it's pretty clear they never meant that these adaptations were "good for business." They simply meant those shifts were "good for wealthy business owners." When certain changes excite business owners only when they stand to benefit exclusively, that means the changes should not be pursued at all. And in that way, a Citizen Dividend may slow unnecessary change.

## It Inspires Common Care for Economic Growth

We want a society where businesses that make profits and benefit the community can thrive. But we also know that many Americans are deeply skeptical of business. According to Gallup research, a majority of Americans believe large US companies do a poor or very poor job at "grow[ing] the . . . economy," "creating good jobs for Americans," and "balancing the best interests of Americans with the best interests of the company."[7] What we don't want, therefore, is a society that is already growing skeptical of business to ignore real concerns business owners may have about policies that choke off their growth. In New York City, nearly a third of all businesses reported it took them over six months to get the city permits they needed to open.[8] In Chicago, a small business shared it had to make thirty-three different tax payments a year to operate.[9] Across the country, nearly 30 percent of all workers need a government-issued license to operate.[10] Determining how to best regulate business is complex. I don't know what the right level of oversight is. But I don't want a population that is so skeptical of business leaders' motivations—or so doubtful of the benefits businesses provide society—that we fail to meaningfully address any constraints to growth that ineffective regulations may pose on businesses.

The Citizen Dividend would tie the benefits of economic growth more closely to the wallets of everyday Americans. The right pro-growth and probusiness policies and regulations would directly benefit the bottom line of every American household. Therefore, we can mitigate resentment against businesses that thrive by disbursing some of their profits to us citizens.

As with all aspects of this proposal, the Citizen Dividend is not a panacea to address the skepticism and mistrust many Americans have with big business. Participating in their profits will not and should not make Americans less willing to hold businesses to a high standard regarding how they treat employees, communities, customers, and the environment. But participating in their profits will make more Americans more willing to get behind policies that support thoughtful economic growth.

## It Connects Us to One Another

Beyond more tightly weaving the connection between business leaders and everyday Americans, a Citizen Dividend has the potential to bind Americans more tightly to one another. We have seen many of the ways that economic and political rifts between Americans are widening. We also see a stark divide between rural and urban Americans. The disdain that emerges from this divide is often personalized.

This resentment is frequently a two-way street. Rural suspicion of mainstream media and urban power is matched by cosmopolitans' mistrust of what they view as the hinterlands. Arlie Russell

Hochschild, whose book *Strangers in Their Own Land* was discussed in an earlier chapter, calls out both conservatives' anger with perceived "line cutters" supported by coastal elites and liberals' frustration with the "stupid rednecks" who threw our collective lot in with Trump and want to make America go backward.

A Citizen Dividend is not a cure to all that divides us. Our divisions go back decades and sometimes centuries. In my home state of Illinois, we see that rift between "downstate" Illinoisans and Chicagoans. Savvy politicians inflame the resentment of people living outside of Chicagoland with (often false) claims that the big city drains more public resources than it contributes. But the Citizen Dividend can mitigate the widening of the rift. If downstate citizens tangibly and directly benefit from the economic powerhouse of Chicago and Chicagoans recognize a concrete benefit from the agricultural and manufacturing industries of downstate, Illinoisans may appreciate that the people who live in those other areas might not be half bad. Or at least, even if it isn't enough to alleviate deep-seated resentment, it would remind us all that we are tied to one another. If our Citizen Dividend comes to us each year because of the hard work of the immigrant, the city resident, *and* the farmer, then even if someone resents people from other groups, they must acknowledge that their own (economic) well-being is connected to the work of people in them.

### It Reinforces Our American Values

Perhaps the most important reason the Citizen Dividend matters is that it reflects our American value of pulling together. Now that we have been a country for almost 250 years, it is easy to forget how distinct the colonies were from one another. They were founded in different ways at various times, led by diverse types of leaders, and bolstered by different economies. And yet this ragtag group came together, acknowledged their dream of a common future, and formed something never seen in world history. This was the real revolution. It was a revolution not just of arms but of values and ideas.

There have been many times in our history when forces from within have tried to convince us that we should embolden our separateness from one another—during the Civil War, the Jim Crow South, and nativist movements in the West and North. But each time, e pluribus unum prevailed. We proved over and over again that we are not a country whose strength rests in our distinctions from one another. Our greatness lies in our willingness to pull together across our differences.

We are living in a time when our economic system is reinforcing our separateness. New income is being retained by those who are already at the top, and wealth is being hoarded by those who are already rich. But the Citizen Dividend—as modest a proposal and as small a payment as it is—reinforces a contrasting story, a story that claims we all play a role in the creation of wealth and value. A story that reminds us that what we own together plays an important part in the creation of profits.

To the entrepreneurs, the CEOs, and the investors: Keep your 95 percent. Use it to pay taxes, to save, to reinvest, to spend. But return a small fraction to the joint owners of the wealth you used to help make that profit.

The Citizen Dividend reminds us, in our uniquely American way, that no matter what state we live in, no matter what the condition of our local economy, no matter who our leaders are, no matter where we were born or what we do for a living, we all share the burdens and the benefits of bolstering our economy and our society. Regardless of any other concrete gain, this realignment with our American values is the most critical reason we must have a Citizen Dividend.

# 12

# WHAT A CITIZEN DIVIDEND IS NOT

Every proposal—even one as modest, albeit far-reaching, as the Citizen Dividend—is bound to bring out the detractors. Long ago, I learned that there are many who believe the surest way to appear smart is to reject the possibility of changing the status quo. Critical thinking is often confused with being critical.

I think a healthy debate on the Citizen Dividend is good. Lively discussion will make the proposal better. Over time it will broaden the buy-in for the dividend among more and more groups. In order to foster the most productive debate, though, we must first focus the conversation. By being honest about what the Citizen Dividend is *not*, we can have a deeper debate on what the Citizen Dividend can and should be.

## A Citizen Dividend Is Not a Tax

Any attempt to increase what businesses may have to pay back to society often runs headfirst into the oft-recited objection that the United States already has the highest corporate tax rate in the developed world. Before moving on, let's be clear that this objection is simply not true, especially when you take into account all the tax deductions and tax loopholes we allow companies to take advantage of. In 2017, when former US House Speaker Paul Ryan was complaining about high corporate taxes as he was shepherding a massive tax cut bill through Congress, the US ranked fourth among Organisation for Economic Co-operation and Development (OECD) countries in its effective corporate tax rate, behind Argentina, Japan, and the UK and only slightly ahead of Germany.[1] Since the 2017 tax bill became effective, the US doesn't even rank among the top ten countries in the OECD with the highest corporate tax rates.[2] Despite complaints to the contrary, US corporations are not burdened with higher taxes than many of our peer countries.

With that out of the way, it is important to clarify that the Citizen Dividend is not a tax. The government does not collect the dividend payments in order to spend them on public services. Public services are essential. A robust military, a solid infrastructure system, good public schools, and a reliable energy grid are all valid expenses for a government. These investments are critical for our society and our economy to function. But the government does not collect the Citizen Dividend to pay for these services. Rather, the Citizen Dividend comes from the private sector and immediately returns to the private sector. Recipients of the dividend can use it immediately as they see fit. They can save it for a rainy day, spend it to bolster the economy, or invest it for growth. For those who oppose higher tax rates due to a fear that it takes money away from the private sector, realize this truth: the money that goes to the Citizen Dividend never really leaves the private sector.

## A Citizen Dividend Is Not Big Government

I understand where our national skepticism toward robust government comes from. After all, our nation was founded after overthrowing a distant and tyrannical ruler. Many nineteenth-century Americans moved West to "settle" the land and make a future for themselves without the everyday presence of a strong government.

But I have always found this national antigovernment narrative confounding. As the son of an army officer, for most of my childhood, I lived in communities where the government built and provided housing, schools, health care, and infrastructure for my family and the families around us. It was a happy childhood where everyone's basic needs were met.

But I also find the antigovernment narrative confounding in part because it ignores the reality of US history. It overlooks how government has acted intentionally in many ways to enrich those with power or those who share identity with those in power. Land grants, zoning, selective law enforcement, state-backed loans, and preferential financing are simply a few examples. Over and over again we have used the power of government to benefit some and exclude others, often on the basis of race. The result is that those who do not share an identity with those in power have to fight twice as hard for half the benefits.

But finally, I find the antigovernment narrative confounding because it is often taken to a counterproductive extreme. *This American Life*—the great radio program produced out of WBEZ in Chicago—ran a powerful story unpacking what happened in Colorado Springs following the 2008 market collapse.[3] A town that had relied on tourism for a major source of revenue now found itself running huge deficits just to keep city services running. The city council members had a choice: they could either raise taxes or cut services. If they raised property taxes so that the average home-owner paid just $200 more per year, they could maintain their full level of services. The city council put it to the people. The voters rejected the referendum by a two-to-one margin.

But then the city did something truly unheard of. They began allowing citizens to purchase services à la carte. To have the street-lights turned on in front of your house for the year, for example, cost $300. When City Councilwoman Jan Martin asked a man why he paid $300 to have his streetlights turned on but voted down a tax of $200 to give him all his city services, his response was simply that he "would never support a tax increase." This resistance to govern-ment providing a robust suite of community services is not only counterproductive. It is expensive.

Despite my full support for high-quality government services that make our community lives better, the Citizen Dividend is not more government. It is a direct payment from creators of value (businesses) to co-owners of the wealth used to create that value (citi-zens). It barely passes through the government at all. It is not funded through annual legislative negotiations. It does not require a tax-funded bureaucracy. It does not rise and fall based on the whims of legislative negotiations or executive orders. It does not increase the size of government payroll. It does not create long-term financial liabilities for the public to bear.

Although the dividend's collection and distribution is enforced by the government, it is otherwise completely separate and distinct. It is a manifestation of the belief in the market and the private sector. It simply recognizes a basic concept of investment: when people pour their wealth into a venture to create value, those inves-tors should share in that value.

I will go even further and point out that a Citizen Dividend is a doubling down on the private sector, not a turn toward social-ism. I remember the monochromatic existence of the former East

German town of Oberwiesenthal. I remember how basic needs—but not much else—appeared to have been met. A Citizen Dividend is a turn away from socialism and government-run enterprises. No businesses are nationalized. Decisions about how businesses are run remain in the hands of private individuals.

Thoughtful debate about the size and scope of government is essential. But as a payment between private citizens, the Citizen Dividend falls outside that debate.

## A Citizen Dividend Is Not Wealth Redistribution

Some may bring up the bogeyman of "wealth redistribution" to attack the Citizen Dividend. Taking on this critique is a bit like shadowboxing a shape-shifter. Critics almost always use the slur selectively, to mean the transfer of wealth from someone they value to someone they don't. They don't call it "wealth redistribution" when Fred Trump passes down an inheritance to Donald Trump—wealth Donald did not work for or earn in the market sense. They don't call it "wealth redistribution" when Warren Buffet collects a dividend payment from a company he invests in. "Wealth redistribution" is usually meant to lambast the transfer of wealth from the rich to the poor, not from one rich person to another rich person.

In fairness to those who put forth the argument in good faith, "wealth distribution" can be a critique of the compelled transfer of wealth among private parties. If Fred Trump wants to give money to Donald, so be it, they say. If the board of American Airlines votes to distribute a dividend to shareholders, including Warren Buffett, so be it. But when government compels the transfer of wealth from one person to another, free market thinkers get skittish.

At its premise though, the bogeyman of "wealth redistribution" supposes that the way we currently allow businesses to structure themselves, how we define profits, and who gets to claim ownership in these profits are all fixed, if not ideal. When profits are claimed by executives and investors, the flow of wealth is "appropriate." But when the same profits are taxed to fund social programs or otherwise distributed to a broader base of people, critics cry out "wealth redistribution." In both cases, profits are going from the business to individuals, but only certain people are deemed worthy to claim these profits. It is almost as if the doomsayers of "wealth redistribution" believe that business structures such as limited liability companies (LLCs) and corporations exist in nature in their ideal form, untouched by human decision-making. Any compelled transfer of the profits that flow from them, they argue, is unwise at best and unjust at worse.

But we were not given our modern notions of ownership and profit from a sacred deity. We created them over the course of centuries to distribute profits to people we think deserve them. So when we recognize the limits of our thinking and understand that the structures we have devised to pass wealth along are human and provisional, we see that we are free to adjust them without fearing that doing so is a threat to either private ownership or capitalism. To acknowledge that we all own some key resources together and equally is not an affront to the concept of private ownership; it is merely a deeper and more true understanding of all the factors that go into wealth creation. And when we use our democratic institutions to make sure that the payouts from wealth creation accrue to all owners of the assets used in creating that wealth, we act consistently with the market frameworks we have inherited. After all, a Citizen Dividend is merely the transfer of value from producers to owners. Such transfers are a bedrock principle of free market capitalism.

## A Citizen Dividend Is Not a Social Benefit Program

We have tackled the initial objections many on the right will make. It is not a tax. It is not big government. It is not wealth redistribution. On the other side of the aisle, many on the left may oppose the Citizen Dividend because it doesn't do enough to tackle poverty. Why build up a social benefit program, they may argue, that provides the same funds to Bill Gates and an out-of-work single mom in rural Appalachia?

Benefits like the Supplemental Nutrition Assistance Program (SNAP), housing assistance, Medicaid, and the Earned Income Tax Credit (EITC) make our society better by directing targeted resources to those most harmed by the injustices of our economy. We need these robust social benefit programs. We need broader access to health care so that people's wealth does not dictate their health. We need better routes to higher education without crushing student debt. We need broader housing security so that no one has to worry over where their child will sleep at night. Justice demands we take better care of our most vulnerable. But even beyond justice, we are all safer, richer, and healthier as a society when we reduce poverty's crushing harms.

But the Citizen Dividend is not a social benefit program; it is a right. And no one in our society is due more rights than anyone else. No one is due a greater vote or more free speech or more religious freedom because of their need. Rich and poor alike have equal rights to life, liberty, and the pursuit of happiness.

Enacting a Citizen Dividend will make our society better. Even though everyone will receive the same amount, that amount will benefit most those who need the additional cash. But the Citizen Dividend is not an antipoverty program. There are better means for accomplishing that worthy objective.

Let's do more to eliminate poverty and the debilitating toll it exacts on families across our country. We can implement the Citizen Dividend and build a stronger social safety net simultaneously. A robust Citizen Dividend program, which acknowledges that we are all bound together, may even help strengthen the national political will to take better care of our most vulnerable.

The Citizen Dividend flows from the acknowledgment that wealth we all own together is being used to create value. That equal ownership is the basis for the dividend. The poor do not own a greater share of our natural resources, and the rich do not own a greater share of our Constitution. The Citizen Dividend is a right we all hold equally. We should therefore all benefit equally.

## A Citizen Dividend Is Not a Universal Basic Income

The conversation about a universal basic income (UBI) has been heating up over the past few years. The debate has moved from the policy fringes to mainstream media. One Sunday morning in spring, as my husband and I sipped coffee on the couch, we turned on CBS *Sunday Morning* to see a story about a UBI experiment in Stockton, California. By the time a concept gets covered on CBS *Sunday Morning*, it is not a fringe idea anymore. We'll see in the next chapter a bit more about what happened in Stockton.

The concept of a universal basic income is that every person in a society will receive the necessary income needed to live—the income needed to cover food and shelter and health care and foundational life expenses—regardless of work. For a superb detailing of the reasons this makes sense and how it might be implemented, I recommend labor leader Andy Stern's book *Raising the Floor*.[4] With data about the dynamism of our current economy and stories of how the many rapid changes in our economy are leaving too many people in the lurch, Stern makes a compelling case for why we should consider a UBI.

Proponents of a universal basic income argue it is essential on three fronts. First, it inoculates individuals from the shocks of a volatile economy. As we've seen, globalization, automation, and technological advancements may strengthen our economies over time, but they wreak havoc on various communities in the short term. With a UBI, these forces can continue without strong political opposition because they won't deprive people of the income they need to survive.

Second, a UBI reduces inefficient government spending on welfare. Large, complex bureaucracies are needed to administer programs such as food stamps and unemployment insurance and even Social Security, because the government has to make sure that those receiving the benefits are in fact eligible for them. When the government doesn't have to administer those large bureaucracies, it can funnel more dollars directly into the hands of people.

Third, having a UBI makes work more productive. When people's most basic needs are met, they can in turn work on what is most beneficial to them and society. No longer would the next groundbreaking artist, great American novelist, or inventor of a groundbreaking new technology have to divert forty to sixty hours of their work per week to something else just to have their needs met. They now can spend their time working on what is most valuable.

Despite the many ways I am compelled by the arguments for some form of universal income, the Citizen Dividend is not a UBI. Admittedly, it is universal in the sense that every citizen will receive a share of the wealth. But it is not currently intended to meet the basic needs of any person or household. The dividend level I propose is modest. It is not nearly enough to cover the cost of food, shelter, clothing, and all the other basic needs that someone has today. Furthermore, unlike a UBI, which most proposals suggest will remain relatively constant each year, the dividend will fluctuate annually with the strength of the economy. When businesses are turning a profit, it will go up. When they are suffering losses, the dividend will shrink. There is no expectation that the dividend will remain at a level sufficient to provide for a person's or household's basic needs. A Citizen Dividend won't eliminate the need for work.

If the Citizen Dividend proves as successful as I believe it could be, and if society's rapid economic changes bring about a swelling public demand for a UBI, the dividend could be the mechanism by which we explore the delivery of that UBI. After all, we will already have a structure that collects wealth created by our national economic prosperity and delivers it to everyone. But at this point, the Citizen Dividend is not designed to meet that ambitious objective.

———

Coming across the proposal for the Citizen Dividend for the first time, we are likely to see it through the lens of what we are most familiar with. Those who have spent a career steeped in debates over taxation and government social programs may evaluate the Citizen Dividend as they would judge a new tax proposal or housing program. Those who have devoted their work to discussions about the merits of wealth redistribution may dig up those arguments to defend or reject aspects of the Citizen Dividend. The new wave of thinkers who are wrestling with the call for a universal basic income may assess the Citizen Dividend against the criteria they have for supporting or opposing UBI. But it is important to focus the discussion of a Citizen Dividend by being honest about what it is not. Only then can we truly come to terms with what it could be.

# 13

# BUILDING OFF OTHER AMERICAN EXPERIMENTS

We learned in the last chapter that the Citizen Dividend is not like the other programs or incentives most of us know well; it's in a category of its own. But just because a Citizen Dividend is unlike other familiar programs, that does not mean it is entirely without precedent. In fact, a number of similar initiatives have arisen across America over the past few decades, and these can help us glimpse the possibilities ahead.

## The Alaska Permanent Fund

Jay Hammond liked to describe himself as a bush rat. Born in upstate New York, he served as a marine pilot in World War II before settling in Naknek, Alaska, a town of a few hundred people nestled into the point where the Aleutian Peninsula begins its five-hundred-mile jut into the Bering Sea. Like many Alaskans, he wore multiple hats. He was a wildlife officer, a pilot, a trapper, and eventually Alaska's fourth governor. But he liked the self-effacing descriptor so much that he titled his autobiography *Tales of Alaska's Bush Rat Governor*.[1]

When Alaska gained statehood in 1959, it had fewer than 250,000 residents. Many were like Jay Hammond, drawn by the wilderness, opportunity, and remoteness of this northern frontier. Take the population of Boise, Idaho, and drop them in an area the size of France and you can begin to get a sense of the sparseness that lured Hammond north.

In those early years of statehood, things were rough going. The local economy was anemic. Roughly half the workforce was employed by the federal government, mostly in the military. Fishing, logging, and mining employed many of the rest.[2] Hammond was recruited—reluctantly, he claims—to serve in Alaska's first state legislature, where he ended up working almost continuously for nearly fifteen years. During that time, he saw how outside interests gained enormously from Alaska's resources. In his own greater Bristol Bay community, he estimated that only 3 percent of the value of the fishing industry was returned to local residents. His community was poor and lacked many of the basic services that those in the lower forty-eight states had. Hammond pointed out that Bristol Bay had "no sewer or water systems. No municipal light or power. . . . No police. No firefighters. . . . Not even designated garbage dumps."[3] And yet they sat on the shores of a treasure chest. Outside interests caught their riches and hauled them away, with little return to the people who called the waters home.

In response, in 1965, he sought to create Bristol Bay, Inc. He proposed increasing the tax that fish processors and fishers paid on each fish caught in Bristol Bay, with the payments going to a fund that would be managed professionally. While 50 percent of the fund's annual return would go to paying for community services (e.g., schools), the remaining 50 percent would be paid out to the individual residents of greater Bristol Bay.

The voters didn't buy it—a reluctance due, Hammond believed, to his "garbled message" on the issue. Hammond remained frustrated as he watched the value of his community's natural resources flow with abandon out of his community.

Three years later, in 1968, the largest oil field in North America was discovered on the far side of the state from Bristol Bay, in northern Alaska's remote Prudhoe Bay. When the state leased the drilling rights to Prudhoe Bay in 1969, it brought in $900 million in a single day, which was nine times the state's budget the previous year.[4] A few voices, including Jay Hammond, argued for setting aside some of the windfall as a "nest egg" for the future. But Alaska was a new state, and a heavily rural one at that, and the need for investment was high. There was a sense that Alaska had a good deal of "catching up" to do to ensure its residents had access to many of the same basic services as other states. The building of a Trans-Alaskan Pipeline System, which would pump the Prudhoe Bay oil to Valdez on Alaska's southern shores and eventually out to the world, was underway, after all. The popular idea of the day held that the $900 million would tide the state over until oil started to flow. Then revenue from oil excise taxes would seamlessly replace the revenue from the lease.

But delays to the Trans-Alaskan Pipeline System's construction were ongoing. The lure of investing the lease revenue into capital projects and a few key state programs proved too much. By 1975, the original $900 million had been fully spent, and oil and its excise taxes weren't expected to flow until at least 1977.[5]

This problem landed squarely in the lap of Republican Jay Hammond, who in 1974 had won a long shot bid to oust a Democrat incumbent and become Alaska's governor. Building on his years of frustration in seeing outsiders hoard almost all of the benefits from Alaska's natural resources, he was similarly dismayed that his Cassandra-like pleas to set aside some of the original $900 million into a reserve fund had been ignored. Hammond believed that too much of the value of Alaska's natural resources left the state, and the little that was retained for its benefit was being imprudently managed by spendthrift politicians.

He decided to pitch his idea of an Alaska Permanent Fund, which was similar to his original Bristol Bay, Inc. proposal. The state would place oil excise taxes into a permanent fund. It would then distribute a portion of all returns on this fund to Alaskans in the form of a cash payment each year. To establish such a fund would require amending the state's constitution, so Hammond traveled throughout Alaska to promote the idea. In 1976, voters approved a constitutional amendment to create the fund by a margin of two to one.

This amendment required the state to place 25 percent of all payments from oil, gas, and mineral royalties and taxes into a fund whose principal could not be spent but whose investment income would be made available to use by the state. In 1980, the Alaska state legislature approved a dividend program that would require an annual distribution to Alaska residents, paid from earnings on the fund. After it was tweaked and survived a state legal battle, it issued its first distribution of $1,000 per resident in 1982.

As it works today, each year the dividend is established by taking roughly half of the average annual income of the fund over the previous five years, subtracting administrative costs, and dividing the remainder up among the number of Alaska residents, including children.[6] Since that first distribution, it has doled out a payment every year to Alaskans from a low of $331 in 1984 to a high of $3,200 in 2008. As of 2019, the value of the underlying Alaska Permanent Fund topped $64 billion, meaning that each Alaskan received $1,606 from the fund, which amounted to $6,424 for a family of four.[7]

As Hammond saw it, the fund and its annual dividend work for three key reasons. First, Alaskans receive an actual payment. Prior to the Alaska Permanent Fund, Hammond had secured passage of an "energy tax credit," funded by an increase in the gas severance tax. This credit was applied to state residents' tax liability, thereby reducing their tax bills by $150 annually. Following its implementation, Hammond was surprised to hear that residents knew little about this credit they were receiving. From this, he learned that for voters to fully appreciate the benefits of the Alaska Permanent Fund dividend, they would have to receive a concrete payment, not merely a reduction in their tax bills.

Second, the dividend payment is paid out equally to all residents. In fairness, this was not how Hammond originally envisioned the dividend program. He wanted the state to issue one "stock" to each Alaskan for every year of residency and pay out the dividend on the basis of that stock. The result would be that the longer that people lived in Alaska, the bigger their payment would be each year. However, this design was struck down by the US Supreme Court as a violation of the US Constitution's Equal Protection Clause. The state legislature redesigned the dividend program so that every Alaskan receives an equal payment every year, regardless of how many years they have lived in the state. While this is not what Hammond wanted, in hindsight he conceded that by ensuring every Alaskan is an equal shareholder, the constituency that supported the fund and its dividend payment was strengthened. It would be impossible for future politicians to play some Alaskans off others in tinkering with the fund.

Finally, the fund payment is structured as a right, not a benefit. Alaska's constitution directed the state to manage its natural resources as a type of public trust "for the maximum benefit of its people." This gave Alaskans the unique ability to impose such a program because, Hammond believed, it acknowledged that the people—not the state government—owned Alaska's rich natural resources. To counter the claims that such a program was socialism or a redistribution of wealth, Hammond pointed out that "socialism is government taking *from* a wealthy few to provide what government thinks is best for all. The Permanent Fund dividends do just the opposite. They take . . . money which . . . belongs to all and allows each individual to determine how to spend some of his or her share."[8] Even small-government champions like Alaska governor and Republican vice-presidential candidate Sarah Palin described the annual payments as "returning a share of resource development dollars back to the people who own the resources."[9] This was not government spending or a bloated public welfare program, according to Republicans like Hammond and Palin, but a return to the people of money that rightly belongs to them.

Today, the Alaska Permanent Fund is popular and has had a meaningful impact on the lives of state residents. In 2017, 40 percent of Alaskans said the annual payments made a "great deal" or "quite a bit" of difference in their lives. Additionally, 72 percent of them supported the fact that the fund payment was distributed to every Alaskan.[10]

For nearly forty years in the United States, an annual distribution to citizens has existed. The program was put into place by a Republican governor and supported by a people largely distrustful of government taxation and spending. Today, Alaska's annual dividend payment is viable, popular, and effective.

### The Eastern Band of Cherokee Indians and Per-Capita Payments

It takes me just over an hour to drive from Asheville west to Cherokee, North Carolina. The last twenty-five minutes take me up and over the Soco Gap on a curvy two-lane road. During this climb and descent, I have no cell coverage. I am amazed that Google

Maps still knows where I am. As I wind my way into town, I pass a number of churches and roadside craft vendors. And then all of a sudden, I turn a bend and a twenty-one-story building reaches upward. One might think it would be out of place in this rolling forest country, but the brilliant windows bordered by a tree-bark-brown frame reflect back the blue sky and green mountainside. It is remarkably beautiful. This is the Harrah's Cherokee Casino, the primary employer and economic engine of the town and of the Eastern Band of Cherokee Indians.

The Eastern Band formed out of tragedy. The Indian Removal Act of 1830 authorized President Andrew Jackson to implement the forced resettlement of tens of thousands of Native Americans from the Appalachian Mountains westward. We now know this militarized death march—in which over ten thousand Native Americans died—as the Trail of Tears. A group of eight hundred Cherokee resisted the resettlement. After their leader, Tsali, was captured and executed, the remaining tribe members were allowed to stay in exchange for giving up their tribal citizenship. Later, in the early twentieth century, their descendants reorganized, and the US government granted them federal recognition as the Eastern Band of Cherokee Indians. They still call the Qualla Boundary—an eighty-square-mile region in the western tip of North Carolina—home.

In 1988, the United States Congress passed the Indian Gaming Regulatory Act (IGRA) to legalize and regulate gaming on tribal lands. Tourist revenue had been a big driver of the local economy in Qualla, but by the 1980s, increased competition from other regional attractions was siphoning off tourist dollars. To respond to this threat, the tribal council of the Eastern Band petitioned the state government in 1991 for the right to open a casino pursuant to the IGRA. The petition was met with widespread opposition. The state government stonewalled. Many local tribe members feared the moral, cultural, and social hazards of legalized gambling. The internal fight within the tribe was intense, with accusations of fraud, corruption, and double-dealing. After years of negotiations with the state, within the tribe, and with various casinos, Harrah's Cherokee Casino opened in 1997.

Perhaps most remarkably, the tribe determined that 50 percent of the profits it received from the casino would be distributed annually or biannually to every member of the roughly fourteen-thousand-person tribe, whether they lived on the reservation or not.[11] The other half of the profits would go to fund "social programs and construction projects on the reservation."[12]

In the first few years, the annual per-capita payments were less than $2,000.[13] Since then, however, they have grown substantially. In 2019, the EBCI Treasury announced its largest per-capita payments: over $13,000 per member.[14]

I wanted to know what the impact of these payments had been, so I figured I should start by reaching out to the person at the top.

Richard Sneed is the principal chief of the Eastern Band.[15] He was born in Cherokee in 1967 but spent big chunks of his youth away from home, living with his mother in New Jersey before coming back to Cherokee as a teen. Later as a young man, he served in the Marine Corps. This time away and back has given him an opportunity to see issues facing the tribe from both an inside and outside perspective. Prior to becoming chief, he was an esteemed teacher and had earned the honor of the National Indian Education Association's Teacher of the Year award in 2013. His success as a teacher helps explain why it is so easy to learn from him. He is patient, quick to offer examples, and always ready to explain.

Chief Sneed sees many benefits to the per-capita payment system. First, the basic quality of life for most tribal members has improved under the program. Housing is probably the easiest way to illustrate this change. When Chief Sneed was a teenager, the valley was dotted with "single wide trailers and project homes that were built by HUD funds." Now "people live in nice homes that you would see in a suburban neighborhood somewhere."

Second, as an educator, he appreciates the investment in the tribe's human capital. Young people, thanks to their per-capita payments and tribal support, can afford tuition, housing, meals, books, and other educational materials. Cherokee youth have the opportunity to invest in themselves and their future in a way they didn't when Chief Sneed was graduating from high school.

Research from Duke University professor Jane Costello confirms much of what Chief Sneed has concluded through anecdotal evidence. The per-capita payments have had a tremendous impact on the well-being of children in the EBCI. She compared various outcomes among the Cherokee children in families receiving the distribution to rural white non-Cherokee children in the same community. The children from the poorest Cherokee families saw behavioral problems decline by 40 percent. And over time, children in Cherokee families were one-third less likely to develop substance abuse or psychological problems as young adults.[16] Perhaps an even more fascinating finding is that young Cherokee men who were receiving the per-capita payments became more optimistic about their future. Using an assessment called "self-reported life span," which measures how long individuals believe they will continue to live, researchers reported young Cherokee men had a fifteen-year increase in their self-reported expected life span compared to similarly situated white peers who had not received the payments.[17] The payments literally made recipients more hopeful about their future.

But Chief Sneed cautions that the story isn't all roses. First, he worries about a unique component of the Cherokee per-capita payment: the Minor's Trust Fund. Each year, children under the age of eighteen have their per-capita payment deposited into a trust fund set up for their benefit. At eighteen, they get full access to that fund. Chief Sneed worries it is too much at one time for young people. When he first started teaching in 2003, he remembers eighteen-year-olds coming into $50,000. Today, young people are getting access to over $100,000 all at once. And many of them spend it the way any eighteen-year-old would spend an enormous windfall: irresponsibly.

Second, he worries that if the per-capita payments are too high, it will create a culture of dependency. He is particularly sensitive to this given the way the US government has treated Native peoples for the past century and a half. The US government "viewed [Native Americans] as little children, as domestic dependents," he says, flushing with anger as he recalls this history. "Natives were rounded up, put on reservations, and in most cases [became] completely dependent upon federal aid to subsist because their way of life and their way of existing and caring for themselves had been stripped away from them." He believes in the per-capita payment, but he wants to ensure it doesn't continue an anti-Indigenous trend of denying people their agency.

Finally, he points out that per-capita payments are not a panacea for all society's problems. Dumping money into parts of a community that are unhealthy without addressing the underlying issues can wreak havoc. For example, when the previous chief started a loan program, whereby tribal members could take out a monthly loan backed by their next per-capita payment, parts of the community suffered. "As soon as the loan program started," Chief Sneed shares, "breaking and entering and petty larceny, petty theft went down by 50 percent. [But] every month on check day, drug trafficking went up and overdoses went up. . . . All we were doing was fueling the drug economy with the loan program." Giving money to people who are harmed and unhealthy because of unaddressed inequities in the broader community doesn't rectify those inequities. Sometimes, it exacerbates their impact.

At the end of the day, Chief Sneed is supportive of the per-capita payments program even though he believes it needs some significant adjustments. "We today as Cherokees have enjoyed great benefits because of the perseverance of our ancestors. Let us never forget that there was a price paid for us to enjoy the benefits we enjoy today." But, he continues, the per-capita payments are a "benefit. I don't see them as a right. They can be taken away for whatever reason . . . because there's not [enough] money [or] because it's determined [by the tribal council] not to be a good program."

I am sensitive to Chief Sneed's deep concern about perpetuating dependency and caution about not viewing guaranteed payments from shared wealth as a right. A right exists in good times and in bad, whether you earn it or not. A benefit fluctuates. It can be earned or taken away. And I agree a specific per-capita payment amount, like a specific Citizen Dividend distribution amount, is not guaranteed. The level that is paid out is a benefit. However, the *source* of that benefit is a right. Tribal members have a right to the disbursement of profits from their shared wealth. That disbursement may be zero dollars one day if the casino loses money or gaming dwindles or disappears. But the right still exists, even if the benefits are low. As Chief Sneed teaches me, "Natural resources, human resources, economic resources, in our case, [all] belong to the collective."

## Guaranteed Income Pilots in Stockton and Jackson

We already know the Citizen Dividend is not a universal basic income (UBI). But there have been some promising results from UBI experiments that we might learn from. They won't help us to understand the impact of tying all Americans together more tightly in a share of our joint economic fortune, but they may shed some light on the impact of consistent nonlabor income on families.

In February 2019, the City of Stockton, California, began giving $500 a month to 125 city residents. Each participant was randomly selected from "neighborhoods with populations that are at or below Stockton's median income level."[18] The initiative—the Stockton Economic Empowerment Demonstration (SEED)—was a coming together of many great minds to test the power of UBI. It was catalyzed by the dynamic young mayor of Stockton, Michael Tubbs. It was funded by the Economic Security Project, which is cochaired by Facebook cofounder Chris Hughes. The evaluation—which compared recipients to a control group who did not receive the payments—was designed and led by Professor Amy Castro Baker of the University of Pennsylvania and Professor Stacia Martin-West of the University of Tennessee.

In a similar 2019 pilot program in Jackson, Mississippi, twenty low-income Black mothers were selected to receive $1,000 a month in cash for a year. This program, the Magnolia Mother's Trust, is beautifully named after the state flower of Mississippi. Aisha Nyandoro spearheads the trust as the CEO of Springboard to Opportunities, a local nonprofit that works with families living in affordable housing to gather the resources and supports "they need to achieve their goals." In this work, Springboard to Opportunities team members describe themselves as "radically resident-driven," meaning they "trust . . . [that residents] know better than anyone else what they need to be successful."[19] So when Nyandoro's stakeholders told her repeatedly that what they needed most was enough cash to liberate them from the onerous workload of addressing "the constant need for survival," she turned to the Economic Security Project for funding and support.

It is still too early to fully learn from these critical UBI pilots, but we can make out two central themes. First, most of the money went to basic needs. In Stockton, nearly 50 percent of the funds went to food and living expenses.[20] In Jackson, transportation and living expenses were the top uses of the funds. And thanks to the $1,000 payments, 100 percent of the Magnolia mothers reported that they had enough money to meet their basic needs.[21] Second, just as Professor Jane Costello found in Cherokee, participants of the Jackson and Stockton programs became more optimistic about their futures. Over 20 percent of the Magnolia Mothers completed their high school education during the pilot, while 100 percent said they felt more hopeful about their future over the next five years. Anecdotal data in Stockton unveil similar increases in positive outlooks about the future.

The early evidence strongly suggests that guaranteed income programs in America work. When American families are given access to nonlabor income consistently over time, they can better meet their basic needs and simultaneously prepare for the future.

———

As our world fell into disarray in the spring of 2020, members of Congress scrambled to support American families and prevent economic collapse. The first stay-at-home order in the US was issued in California on March 19, 2020. The CARES Act, the largest economic stimulus package in US history, was signed into law eight days later.

Part of this massive law was a $300 billion appropriation for one-time cash payments to adults. Most individuals received $1,200, which meant that married couples received $2,400. Phaseouts began when individuals reported $75,000 in adjusted gross income or $150,000 for married couples.

It will take some time to learn how these payments were spent to fully understand their impact. But what we do know is that there are cracks in the American narrative that income should only be earned on labor. Even our ideas around financial returns have been grounded in this narrative. We get Social Security because we worked hard and paid into the system. We earn returns on our 401(k)s and our IRAs because we earned the principal from our work. Even inheritance is often couched in this labor narrative: our parents and grandparents are being rewarded for their labor by being able to pass their assets down to us.

But in the CARES Act, we saw a willingness in this country to invest in one another outside of our individual labor contributions. In Alaska and in Cherokee, we see the possibility of another American narrative around income. Yes, we earn most of our income through our work, but some income is due to us because we are joint owners in something bigger than us. In Jackson and Stockton, the impact of nonlabor income has been remarkable. When people's basic needs are met, they are more hopeful. They are healthier.

We have enough examples to build from. We know we have a willingness to invest in one another when we need to. There hasn't been a more productive time in nearly a century to rethink how our economy rewards all Americans. The time is now to reclaim the soul of the American economy.

# THE PATH FORWARD

# 14

# WHERE WE GO FROM HERE

It always seems impossible until it is done.

—Nelson Mandela

In the spring of 2018, I attended an award presentation hosted by my alma mater's alumni club in Chicago, where I still live. The event was held at the august University Club of Chicago in its Cathedral Hall. The ceiling looms high above, maybe twenty feet up. Stone crests of some of our country's most elite universities adorn the walls. Large windows overlook the beauty of Millennium Park and Lake Michigan.

That night, as the sun was setting and soft light bathed the room, I sat next to a professor from Kellogg, the business school at Northwestern University. I had recently finished reading Andy Stern's *Raising the Floor* and had been working on this project for a few months by that point. I thought getting an outside perspective on the questions this project raised would be insightful.

I shared with him some of the data mentioned earlier. I started with how many jobs now—and how many of our current work tasks—are at risk of automation in the near future. I asked what he thought of that. He scoffed and cited the fact that half of the labor force in America was working in agriculture in 1850, whereas now less than 2 percent do.[1] There has always been disruption, he said, and the economy and society adapt. I then shared with him the statistics around income inequality and how almost all the gains in income have gone to the top echelons, with most Americans experiencing no real income growth whatsoever. He gently rolled his eyes and said that due to advancements in technology, people can now buy more with less. It didn't matter, he argued, what people earned compared to one another. What really mattered was their purchasing power. I prepared to counter with data on what I've called the "great squeeze" and raise more questions, but the evening's speaker rose to the podium and I was blessedly saved from more of the professor's derision.

The professor's complete lack of concern about the dynamics shifting underfoot represented a broader problem. To be in such an esteemed venue and have a tenured university professor dismiss the anxiety borne by middle- and lower-class Americans was jarring. Most people in this country have seen the economic elite accumulate massive wealth while they themselves have experienced no real gains. They have watched business leaders and owners gobble up income while they fear automation and globalization will threaten their own economic futures. To experience all this and then be told that any concern is unwarranted because everything works out in the end captures the breadth of the chasm between ordinary Americans and our economic and social leaders. We have iPhones and the internet now, the professor seemed to suggest, so who cares about rising inequality?

"Let them eat cake" indeed.

But the professor's response was more than callous. It ignored the active ways in which societies force economies to adapt. It is true that 170 years of economic transformations have brought about a massive shift—from a largely agricultural workforce to one geared toward service and high-tech labor. But we as a society have facilitated and supported those transitions. Social Security, Medicare, Medicaid, unemployment insurance, minimum wage laws, OSHA standards, FHA-backed loans, the GI Bill, universal K–12 public education, Pell grants: these are just some of the ways we have protected workers, helped people master the skills required in this new economy, supported them in accumulating wealth, and created a safety net to uphold those who may not master the transition. Societies didn't just adapt on their own. We took proactive steps to orient one another in new and different ways to support this adaptation.

Often, these actions came as a result of painful social and economic reactions to the dysfunction caused by such economic shifts. The Haymarket Affair, the US mine strikes, the Triangle shirtwaist factory fire, the stock market crash and subsequent Great Depression, and World War II were all violent and harrowing events that helped bring about many of these changes. If the standard the professor holds is that we must have riots and crashes and wars before we meaningfully adapt, the future looks bleak indeed.

But I don't think this has to be the case. We can look at the trends playing out before us. We can acknowledge that they are bad for our country and run afoul of our shared values. We can preempt crises to make real change. The Citizen Dividend is not the only solution worth putting into force, nor is it a panacea. But without it—without an economic recognition that ties the profits of the few to the profits of the many—we will continue to run away from our national values until a real breaking point forces a national reckoning. And that reckoning will be more painful than any of us want.

## A Note on Skepticism and Opposition

When I discuss the idea of a Citizen Dividend, even with the most sympathetic ears, the most common pushback I receive is that it will never pass. Skepticism to the possibility that our society would adopt the dividend often stems from the fear of resistance from two potential sources: voters and the business lobby.

### Voters

I have a friend whose kindness and wisdom far outpace mine and who has worked extensively in national politics for over a decade. Over drinks and chips at a favorite local Mexican restaurant recently, he told me that even if the Citizen Dividend were a good idea, it would never pass because Americans vote from their aspirational self-interest. They see themselves as potentially rich one day, he said, and are therefore opposed to calls to "tax the rich."

My friend may be right about this being difficult legislation to pass, but I am not convinced it is due to people's aspirational belief that they will be major shareholders one day and are eager to claim higher profits for themselves when that day comes. Instead, I believe they are skeptical because Americans are distrustful when things don't appear equal on their face. Equality is a fundamental pillar of American democracy. The great tenet "one person, one vote" is the prime example of this. When people are told to pay more, even if they can afford it, many view it as an affront to a core American principle.

A 2017 study lends credence to this hypothesis. Researchers asked two groups of people whether they thought wealthier people should pay higher taxes. In one group, they preceded this question with a "fairness prompt" by asking, "How important is it that the government guarantees equal voting rights?" In the control group, they prefaced the question on higher taxes for the rich with a prompt totally unrelated to the concept of fairness: "How important is it that the United States government celebrates Thanksgiving?" The researchers found that respondents who had been prompted with the fairness question were less likely to say that the wealthy should pay more in taxes than the control group.[2] Americans are less willing to support programs that require some to pay at higher rates than others.

I am a strong proponent of progressive taxation, which means having the rich pay higher taxes. I think it is right to ask those who have benefitted the most to pay the most. But unlike a campaign to "tax the rich more," the Citizen Dividend treats everyone equally. This increases the likelihood that voters will adopt it. In this model, every business from Google to your local factory pays the same dividend rate. And every person, be it Warren Buffett or a father working double shifts to provide for his family, gets the same distribution. That equal treatment is far less challenging for American voters to wrestle with than one that differentiates us.

## Business

Another common pushback to the idea of the Citizen Dividend is the feared implausibility of passing it over the presumed objections of the business lobby, who will balk at having to pay a 5 percent dividend on top of their corporate taxes.

Before I accept that frame for discussion, I want to first point out that the Citizen Dividend is good for business. It ensures that the greater population benefits concretely and directly from policies that promote business and economic growth. When the government reduces overly burdensome red tape or adopts trade policies that allow a business to export more of its goods, everyone's dividend check will increase. This is the surest way to build a base of support for policies that businesses claim are key for their profitability.

But the political and lobbying muscle of America's largest corporations may oppose the Citizen Dividend despite its benefits to business and our society at large. I admit that opposition would not be easy to overcome. But it is not impossible.

In the summer of 1994, I was a rising high school senior working as an intern in the office of Oklahoma congressman Mike Synar.[3] This was the summer in which the Clinton health care plan died. The fundamental core of the bill was a requirement that all employers provide health care for their employees. The energy and money spent to oppose this effort were immense. Everyone debated it—Congress, the media, people in towns throughout America, and even the courts: "To influence the public, more than $50 million was thrown into advertising, most by opponents."[4] In September 1994, after attempts to moderate the proposal, Senate majority leader George Mitchell declared the effort dead. It wasn't until the election of Barack Obama and the push to adopt the Affordable Care Act (ACA) fifteen years later that a meaningful effort to pursue universal health care was revived. And now, in large part due to the limited (albeit important) effectiveness of the ACA and in part because of the pushing of Vermont senator Bernie Sanders, a government-run health care program for everyone (often called "single-payer health care") is now a popular mainstream proposal. In April 2018, a poll by the *Washington Post* and the Kaiser Family Foundation found that a majority of Americans favored a single-payer plan.[5]

If you had told me in the summer of 1994 that twenty-four years later we would have pushed near-universal health care and that a majority of Americans supported an even more transformative overhaul of the health care system, I would have been incredulous. But good ideas, thoughtfully presented and doggedly pursued, can overcome even the most ardent opposition.

I won't pretend to be Pollyanna on this. The road forward on a Citizen Dividend is not a smooth one. The Citizen Dividend will make us stronger as a country and bind us closer to our national identity, but it will require us to persuade powerful parties whose initial reaction will be to resist. In chapter 13, we saw how Jay Hammond brought his idea of the Alaska Permanent Fund to life despite strong opposition at first. I want to share two additional case studies that fuel my sense of hope that a good idea—persuasively shared with as many people as possible—can be granted life.

## Abolishing Slavery in the British Empire

By the mid-eighteenth century, British slave ships were capturing and carrying over forty thousand enslaved Africans across the Atlantic every year.[6] The slave trade made British plantation owners very wealthy, including those absentee landowners who lived in England and served in Parliament. But the plantation owners weren't the only ones who profited. Slave ship owners and slave traders also reaped the benefits. The port city of Liverpool grew immensely because of the slave trade, transforming from a population of five thousand in 1700 to England's third-largest city a century later, with nearly eighty thousand inhabitants.[7] By the early nineteenth century, the market value of enslaved people held by British subjects was equal to 5 percent of the nation's GDP.

In 1785, in the midst of a nation growing rich from the slave trade, Cambridge University student Thomas Clarkson won a prestigious national competition for his essay denouncing slavery. "No custom established among men," he wrote, "was ever more impious."[8] Before then, outside of the Quaker communities, there had been no meaningful national attention to the issue of abolishing the slave trade or emancipating the enslaved. But Clarkson's winning essay set in motion powerful events to eliminate slavery in the British empire fifty years later. While the factors that contributed to slavery's end were complex, we can boil down the events and figures that led to this massive social and economic reordering to a few key ones. Over the years, Clarkson, Quaker allies, formerly enslaved people like Olaudah Equiano, and the parliamentarian William Wilberforce all worked together—in periods of tension and harmony—to bring about abolition.

According to Adam Hochschild's narrative history *Bury the Chains*, the early abolitionists started close to home.[9] They first focused their calls on ending the slave trade, not abolishing slavery entirely. In doing so, they built an early campaign to detail the horrors of the mistreatment of British sailors in the slave trade. The British public was better primed to be sympathetic to the plights of their fellow countrymen than they were to the sorrows of distant Africans.

Having piqued the public's concern, the abolitionists broadened their campaign to include stories of the horrors of slavery. They partnered with potter and businessman Josiah Wedgwood to mass-produce a seal for one group of abolitionists that depicted an African man looking up from his knees, wrists bound in chains, above a banner reading "Am I Not a Man and a Brother?" They also widely distributed the image of the *Brookes* slave ship plan, an illustration showing 450 Africans crammed in a ship hull to be transported across the Atlantic. In 1789, Olaudah Equiano published a memoir detailing his boyhood in Benin, his capture as a ten-year-old and transport across the Atlantic, his servitude on merchant vessels, and his eventual freedom in England. The book became a best seller and was widely read throughout the country.

By 1790, the abolitionists' parliamentary champion William Wilberforce pressured his colleagues to hold public hearings on slavery. For nearly two years, Parliament heard eyewitness accounts of slavery in action, sifted through data on slavery and the slave trade, and studied slave laws in other jurisdictions. To boil down the almost 1,700 pages of testimony to something useful, the abolitionists published an abstract of all the evidence presented in these hearings for review by people throughout England and its colonies.

As the abolitionists documented and distributed stories of the horror of slavery and the slave trade, outside factors helped render the British public—and its parliament—more receptive than they might have been only a few decades prior. First, the plight of those working in exploitative labor conditions moved the British public's heart more than ever before. The near constant involvement of the Crown in foreign wars led to the rise of much-feared "press gangs"—bands of Royal Navy officials who roamed British towns kidnapping young men and forcing them into military duty. Press gangs brought into stark relief the specter of being forcibly removed from one's own life and family and compelled to labor. It was not the same as slavery—conscripts were paid a small wage, and their impressment was not permanent—but still had the effect of heightening sympathy for what slaves might experience. Simultaneously, the rise of industrialization led to mass employment of Britons in mills and factories. The long hours and hazardous working conditions of these places became widely known, adding to the British public's growing wariness of unjust labor practices.

Second, the world outside of Britain unleashed events that made the calls for abolition fall on receptive ears. The American and French revolutions put pressure on the British House of Commons to reexamine its ostensible commitment to the rule of law and rights of man. A series of successful slave revolts in the 1790s culminated in the establishment of the free nation of Haiti in 1804 and challenged the assumption that slavery was appropriate and just. After all, if the formerly enslaved could govern an entire nation, why could they not be free enough to govern their own individual lives? Further slave revolts throughout the Caribbean led to brutal crackdowns. Stories flooded back home of reactionary plantation owners brutalizing English missionaries, fearing they were outsiders bent on inciting rebellion. The British public laid their sympathies with homegrown missionaries over distant slaveholders.

The intense public information campaign led by the abolitionists and the softening of public opinion fueled by global events began to come together. In 1806, Parliament outlawed British subjects from participating in the slave trade with France and its allies. In 1807, Parliament abolished the British slave trade altogether, and in 1833, it passed a law to emancipate the enslaved. On August 1, 1838, all those enslaved in the British Empire were freed. In compensation, the British government paid former owners of enslaved people a total of £20 million—or 40 percent of the treasury's annual revenues.

Let that sink in: in approximately half a century, a large pillar of the British economy that fueled one of the most powerful political lobbies in Great Britain was taken down by a strong message advanced by organized, sustained, and widespread pressure.

## Establishing Social Security in America

The end of the nineteenth century and the beginning of the twentieth saw dramatic shifts in the American economy. First, there was a massive movement of people from agricultural communities to urban centers. In fact, 1920 represented the first time in American history that more people lived in cities than on farms.[10] Second, due to advancements in medicine, sanitation, and nutrition, American life expectancy was rising.[11] As such, seniors needed greater economic support, as they lived longer in retirement. Yet on the eve of the Great Depression, retirement security was a rare phenomenon in America. Pensions for Civil War veterans and their dependents had been a major part of federal spending during the late nineteenth century, accounting for 37 percent of the federal budget in 1894. As these veterans died out, though, the only major pension system that remained in America was employer-sponsored. But this private sector support was sparse. In 1932, only 5 percent of the elderly were receiving a pension.[12] With the stock market crash of 1929 and massive unemployment, the Great Depression only exacerbated the already pressing need for greater retirement security for American seniors.

In 1933, Francis Townsend, a sixty-six-year-old doctor from Long Beach, California, was laid off with little savings and no employment opportunities. One day, he looked out of his window and saw three elderly women picking through trash. The injustice enraged him. He wrote a letter to the editor of the local *Long Beach Press-Telegram* arguing that every American over age sixty in good standing should receive a national pension of $200 per month. He proposed funding this program, the Old Age Revolving Pension Fund, through a 2 percent national sales tax.

Immediately, people gathered together to start "Townsend Clubs" dedicated to pushing for the adoption of a national old-age pension. By 1935, about seven thousand such clubs had formed with over two million total members.[13] In response to rising pressure from Townsend Clubs and other demands for a greater safety net for retirees, President Franklin Roosevelt established the Committee on Economic Security. It was chaired by Secretary of Labor Frances Perkins and had an executive committee of five cabinet-level officials.

By January 1935, after a whirlwind few months, the committee issued its report. The guiding recommendation was that the federal government create a "program of economic security . . . [whose] primary aim [is] the assurance of an adequate income to each human being in childhood, youth, middle age, or old age—in sickness or in health."[14] It then outlined an admittedly piecemeal approach, driven by what the committee viewed as the practical considerations of the day, to provide for economic security in five parts: employment assurance, unemployment compensation, old-age security, security for children, and security for those in ill health. By June, the resulting Social Security Bill had passed both chambers of Congress. Two years after Frances Townsend wrote his initial letter to the editor, President Roosevelt signed Social Security into law on August 14, 1935.[15]

———

What can we learn from these examples? What can the abolition of British slavery, the establishment of American Social Security, and the creation of the Alaska Permanent Fund, covered earlier, each of which took place across different times and places, teach us today? What does it take to get a society to restructure a major part of its economy?

First, these effective calls for reform did more than highlight the benefits of the proposed changes. They each tied themselves to shared community values. Wilberforce and Clarkson saw early success in their campaign when they focused on British sailors before enslaved people. British sailors were easier for British subjects to identify with than Africans from distant lands. Later, Equiano compared the decent treatment he received among Muslim Turks with his shameful treatment by fellow English Christians. Horror stories were important, but they weren't enough on their own; they became a force for change when they were contrasted with the espoused values of Great Britain or its church. Similarly, Townsend's call for social security rested upon people's familiarity with, and protectiveness toward, old age. Every American had an old person in their family. Every American knew that barring disease or tragedy, they too would live past working age. A call for social security was an appeal to take care of themselves and their loved ones. Hammond, too, rooted his call for the Alaska Permanent Fund in a shared commitment to the natural resources of the state. He did not lead with talk of how big a check every resident would earn. He spoke about how the land belonged to all Alaskans, and so they, not outside moneyed interests, should care for and benefit from its bounty.

Second, outside factors made society ripe for change. In early nineteenth-century England, the threat of press gangs increased British sympathies for the victims of forced labor. Factory work made British people sensitive to unjust labor practices. Plantation revolts across the Caribbean and the revolutions in America and France put pressure on the British to examine their beliefs in liberty and human rights. In early twentieth-century America, the economic collapse of the Great Depression led Americans to see firsthand how vulnerable every person was to financial destitution. A call for a national pension issued five years earlier during the Roaring Twenties likely would not have found as fertile soil as it did in the depths of the Depression. The same was true in Alaska: Hammond's initial proposal for a fund for Bristol Bay went nowhere. It took the state government blowing through nearly a billion dollars' worth of oil money in five years for Alaskans to be ready for an idea like the Alaska Permanent Fund dividend program.

Finally, the proponents of change kept at it. Clarkson won his award for his antislavery essay in 1785. Enslaved people didn't claim their freedom throughout the British Empire for another fifty-three years. By comparison, Townsend's idea for an old-age pension brought about change in a few short years, but it involved the work of two million Townsend Club members across the country advocating on a local level. It took Hammond a failed attempt at Bristol

Bay, a successful win in a long shot campaign for governor, a state-wide tour in favor of a constitutional amendment, and even successful court battles to initiate Alaska's dividend program. Change requires persistence.

### Bringing about a Citizen Dividend

The success of these three campaigns helps establish a framework we can use to breathe life into a Citizen Dividend.

First, we must ground our call for the Citizen Dividend in shared values. It is not enough to talk about the benefits of $500 a year. That would be akin to writing a memo about the positive labor outcomes of a Fourth of July holiday. While it might be true, and it may speak to a subset of people, it fails to connect the proposal to the most powerful current: our national identity, the story of who we are.

It is also insufficient to demonize corporate titans and frame the Citizen Dividend as a sort of economic revenge. Sure, whipping up anger at the beneficiaries of our current economic systems will fuel a subset of people, but there are limits there too. While some business leaders and ultrawealthy work tirelessly to expand the system that allows them to hoard wealth, most beneficiaries of that system are just going along. Many Americans, including the top 1 percent, have bought into the false narrative that wealth and income should be squirreled away by those who can get their hands on it. Few of us have been asked to see how individual wealth grows by using collective wealth. Tapping into anger has its place. But fueling this anger at beneficiaries of a system most people take for granted, and many buy into, won't get us over the finish line by itself.

A call for a Citizen Dividend is most persuasive when we also connect it to our shared national story, to our collective values. We should talk about its benefits. We should inspire righteous anger at the injustices of our current system. But most importantly, a Citizen Dividend is a right step for our nation in addressing our economic inequality because it holds to what already makes us exceptional as a country. Our values, our diversity, and our history all point to the greatness of America: our willingness to pull together across our many differences to make one vibrant nation. To right the wrongs we have allowed to seep into our economy, to benefit all of us, we must claim our national heritage: "out of many, one." That is the power of the Citizen Dividend, something we can all hold onto.

Second, the time is now. There has hardly been a moment in the past fifty years where we have been better positioned to put a Citizen Dividend into place. Rising economic inequality has reached a crescendo that most Americans notice and many Americans feel. The economic collapse of 2008 caused many of us to question a system that so blatantly protects the dominant economic caste over the rest of us. But perhaps most importantly, the economic crisis of the 2020 pandemic and the subsequent scramble to prevent an all-out economic meltdown has made us more willing to give people nonlabor income. It has expanded, perhaps temporarily, our sense of who deserves to benefit from decades of prosperity. The conditions are ripe to advance the idea that every American deserves a slice of the pie baked from our collective wealth.

Finally, we must keep at it. As I write in my basement in the dark of 5:00 a.m. most mornings, I can't foretell how long the road to a Citizen Dividend is. I have a laptop, not a crystal ball. I believe it is somewhere between Clarkson's fifty-three years and Townsend's two. But I can say with certainty that it will take persistence. It will take debate and refinement. It will take reaching out to friends in person and over social media. It will take calling and emailing and meeting with our elected officials. It will take letters to the editor and op-eds. It will take all of these efforts, by many of us. Those of us who believe we must sew one another more closely together in the fabric of our nation must do a little bit over and over again.

To inspire such action is the aim of this book. The path forward will take the input and energy of many. The idea of the Citizen Dividend as laid out here must be challenged, tweaked, and strengthened. We must give it a real form in policy and law, then test it and improve upon it. We can develop public support for the dividend, slowly but steadily. It won't start with a groundswell. But we must take on the work of educating the citizenry of our due right to dividends collected from the use of our jointly owned wealth.

———

History is often described as a highway. And indeed, in hindsight, it appears flat and smooth, its direction inevitable. The path looks clear and singular.

But I tend to think of history as a winding gravel road. When you are on it, you are rarely afforded the clarity of where you are headed; you can't often see more than just a few feet ahead. There are times when the path is sunlit and clear, and times when you are shrouded in dense overgrowth and can barely see past the next bend. But importantly, perhaps most importantly, the road is not smooth. It is made up of thousands upon thousands of small stones, which are the courageous and visionary acts of people throughout history. Change is not smooth. Nor is it carved into the landscape by a single person. The countless small but meaningful acts of people determined to change the course of history are what move us forward.

If you believe in our country and are optimistic about a Citizen Dividend, simply speak up and add one more pebble to the gravel road that will get us there.

# 15

# THE HEARTBEAT
# OF A NATION

The debate about who we are as a country often seems to boil down to one fundamental question: Are we primarily the people of the Declaration of Independence or the people of the Constitution?

The Declaration of Independence broke bonds. It was an announcement of a revolt. It opposed tyranny and listed grievances, urging the dissolution of the "political bands which have connected [the colonies] with another." The Constitution, on the other hand, was a coming together. It called for "a more perfect Union." The verbs in the preamble alone are words like *form*, *establish*, *provide*, and *promote*. It is a frame for how we will unite across our geographic and political differences to create one nation. The Constitution's first word is *We*.

I must admit I am partial to the Constitution and am confused by those who characterize our nation solely by the values espoused in the Declaration of Independence. Don't get me wrong: I love the Declaration of Independence, and I honor the claiming of our individual rights. I join the chorus praising our destiny to pursue life and liberty and happiness. The revolution the Declaration of

Independence announced was indeed historic. The repercussions it would unleash throughout the world over centuries is awe-inspiring. But revolts are nothing new in human history. Ask the Athenians and the Nubians and the Maccabees. Look back on the forces of Liu Bang and Spartacus and Francisco Tenamaztle. Since the dawn of human civilization, we have witnessed revolts and revolutions.

The Constitution is something altogether rarer though, almost unique. Its task was to bind us and sustain us for centuries to come. Thirteen disparate colonies had to unite over something bigger than a shared enemy and a common colonial heritage. They had to weave together a new nation. At the heart of this document is a commitment to one another. It is a celebration of our unity.

Our Constitution is our Founders' boldest undertaking, even though it is admittedly imperfect. It did not escape the paradoxes and cruelties of its time. It enshrined the torture of generational enslavement and counted enslaved Black people as three-fifths of a person for purposes of Congressional representation. It denied equal civic dignity to women. It looked askance at the rightful original inhabitants of the land upon which the country grew. But the dream laid out in our Constitution—that we are better when we bind ourselves to one another and forge one nation out of many parts—is our greatest collective aspiration.

While I have my biases, I know that we are people of both the Declaration of Independence and the Constitution. Freedom and togetherness. Liberty and community. Individual rights and a common country. We pull apart from one another under the values of the Declaration of Independence. We come together under the values of the Constitution. Over and over again. This is the beating heart of our nation.

Our economy has been pulling us apart for over half a century. In our race to embrace financial liberty and market autonomy, we have gone too far. We have allowed CEOs to reap income unimaginable to the everyday worker. We have built entire industries obsessed with returning wealth to corporate shareholders over citizens. We have developed a language that fetishizes individual ownership but forgets what we own together. We have rewarded hoarding. We have celebrated our disconnection from one another and turned our backs on the other part of our national identity that honors who we are as a whole.

For hundreds of years we have been living out a radical experiment—that we can come together across differences to form a nation; that we can build a country out of shared values rather than out of shared ethnic or religious heritage. But the fabric of our experiment is fraying. Our economy has changed rapidly, and we have not adapted our legal and political structures alongside those changes. The result is that in a dynamic and increasingly rich economy, wealth is being disproportionately claimed by the few, leaving most of us little in the way of gains.

I love our country. Fiercely. Proudly. But unless we are willing to hold fast to our commitment to the ideals of our nation—that we are strongest when we are tied together—we will lose this democracy. Maybe not tomorrow, or even in this decade or the next, but soon. The loss may not appear cataclysmic in the moment, but we may look back from an age of oligarchy or authoritarianism at this period of time when we could have chosen to keep our democracy but instead let it slip through our fingers.

The Citizen Dividend is not a silver bullet. It will not immediately solve every one of our problems all on its own. But it is a necessary step, grounded in our values and in clear recognition of the wealth we own together, toward reminding us that our democracy relies on us being bound together.

The Citizen Dividend is a start. An important start at that.

It is time to come back together. It is time to address the out-dated assumptions that have gotten us here. It is time to adjust the rules that govern our markets to unite us more tightly. It is time to recognize that to be truly American, our economy must balance our love of individual autonomy with our commitment to one another. It is time that we, the people, have an economy for "We, the People."

It is time.

# ACKNOWLEDGMENTS

## To My Coconspirators

As Krista Tippett teaches us, "The universe is conspiring in our favor even though we may not understand how."[1]

Nearly three years ago, incensed by the rising inequality in a country I love and hooked on an idea to chip away at that injustice, I committed a revolutionary act. At the time, it didn't seem like a big deal, but in hindsight, it was transformative. I promised myself I would sit down for thirty minutes every morning to write—to form the questions and hammer out the answers that had been circling through my mind for over a year. Six months later, this book had its primordial form.

The real magic though happened next. I slowly started reaching out to the people in my world, looking for those who could help me bring this project forth. I didn't know what I was doing. I had no master plan, no charted course. I merely had an idea, a growing conviction, and a ton of questions. What you see today is the product of a web of eager coconspirators who together breathed life into this book. At least once in everyone's life, I hope they experience the joy that comes in saying timidly, "I have an idea," and watching a network of friends and allies rush forth to help usher that idea forward. It is a wonder to behold.

My fear in documenting my gratitude is that I will inadvertently leave someone important out. I have read enough acknowledgments sections to know this is not an uncommon fear, but it still hangs heavy over me. To my friends and colleagues who supported me along the way, thank you. To the person who crosses my mind as I bolt up in bed in the middle of the night a few months from now, I am sorry I forgot to include you here. Please know it is my absentmindedness and not my lack of gratitude that caused the omission.

I'll begin with my teachers. I learned from every researcher, author, and journalist credited in this book. I appreciate all of their hard work and each of their tremendous insights. In addition, Michael Ansara and Patrick Nash shared their expertise with me and pushed me with their questions. I am particularly grateful to Luke Shaefer. Between raising a family, serving as a professor, and working to alleviate the crushing pain of poverty for Michigan families during a cruel pandemic, he carved out time at every inflection point in the development of this book to advise and encourage. His dual talents of wisdom and humility are gifts to the world. They were certainly gifts to me.

To my muses. Nora Antoine, Michael Carrigan, Ben Chin, Mike Espinoza, Mike Johnson, Clete Kiley, Stephanie Morimoto, Jamaal Nelson, Richard Sneed, and Joanna Williams. They blessed me with their time and with their stories. They were brave enough to allow me to see and hold many parts of their lives. It was an honor to bear witness to them. I was given advice not to fall in love with your subjects because it can make it difficult to write about them objectively. But I couldn't escape it. They all are amazing, brave, and kind people who move through the world seeking to make it better. I thank them for allowing their truths to teach others.

To my refiners. Rita Bosworth, Mike Buman, Krupa Desai, Oren Jacobson, Ameya Pawar, Chasse Rehwinkel, and Eric Scroggins. They each read unpolished sections of this book and had both the kindness and the courage to offer unpolished feedback. To Mitch Locin, my superreader. At every stage of this process—from the first chapter to the book proposal to the near final drafts—he willingly stepped in to edit and inform this work. His consistent generosity meant so much to me.

To my champions. Giles Anderson, my agent, and Lil Copan, my editor. They are true believers that good ideas beautifully told have a place in this world. They fought for this book because they trusted in its potential. I am indebted to them for their ability to look at what did not yet exist and see what could be. To Jana Riess, who rolled up her sleeves and did the long hard work of helping bring this book into focus. To Meg Ansara, Carrie Simons, and Evan Stone, who eagerly connected me to luminaries in their networks so that I could learn and refine my thinking.

This book would not have come together had it not been for two people: Peter Barnes and Donna Foote.

Reading Peter Barnes was like taking the red pill. On a predawn run one morning, I listened to an interview between Ezra Klein and Hillary Clinton where they briefly discussed Peter's *With Liberty and Dividends for All*. Before I got to my front door, I ordered the book. When it arrived, I devoured it. I took it with me everywhere, reading it in bars and on the train. For some time, I had been wrestling with my dismay at the nearly unparalleled levels of economic inequality taking shape in our country. *With Liberty and Dividends for All* forced me to challenge the assumptions that undergird our contemporary economy: What do we own? Who deserves to benefit from our country's wealth? Are our current structures the only ones that could rightfully exist? Asking these big questions eventually led me to a vision of a more hopeful future, one that brings us together and honors our national story. I would not have seen this without Peter's book.

If *Our Fair Share* had a midwife, it was Donna Foote. She was the first person I shared my draft writing with. She saw something taking shape and encouraged me to continue. Without her early and enthusiastic support, I might have just shelved the protomanuscript as an interesting project and moved on. But her early cheers spurred me to continue. Donna counseled me along the way. She was the first one who pushed me to seek out the people and stories that could bring the Citizen Dividend to life. I thank Donna for taking a fragile concept and coaching me as I coaxed it out.

I have dedicated this book to my parents for reasons that I hope are clear from the very first chapter. An army officer and a public school teacher, together they taught me that real patriotism begins with love of others, service to community, and pride in our history. They also gave me the incredible gift of seeing so many different parts of our country unfold from our ever-changing front steps. This was the best soil to help my own patriotism take root.

To my husband—my ever-patient and ever-supportive husband. He is my strong foundation and my soft pillow. He tolerated 4:00 a.m. alarms so I could get out of bed and write. He sat through countless hours of my monologues as I recounted research and stories that caught my interest. He celebrated every little win along the way with me. And after I had written tens of thousands of words but still couldn't land on a title, he came up with one in thirty seconds. The words in the book are my own, but the title on the cover announcing this book to the world is his. Somehow, that seems like a pretty good metaphor for our marriage.

Finally, to my beautiful and vibrant daughter who came into the world as this book was taking form. Throughout it all, she deepened my purpose and gave shape to my hope. May she find the courage to love our country and demand its excellence in equal measure.

# NOTES

## CHAPTER 1: OUT OF MANY, ONE

1 Anne Lamott, *Bird by Bird: Some Instructions on Writing and Life* (New York: Anchor Books, 1994), 62.

2 Martin Luther King Jr., "Letter from a Birmingham Jail," April 16, 1963, available at https://www.africa.upenn.edu/Articles_Gen/Letter_Birmingham .html. Last accessed March 31, 2021.

3 Thomas Piketty, Emmanuel Saez, and Gabriel Zucman, *Distributional National Accounts: Methods and Estimates for the United States*, National Bureau of Economic Research (NBER) Working Paper No. 22945, December 2016.

4 Kimberly Amadeo, "US GDP by Year Compared to Recessions and Events: The Strange Ups and Downs of the US Economy since 1929," Balance, August 2, 2018, https://www.thebalance.com/us-gdp-by-year-3305543.

5 US Bureau of Economic Analysis, "Real Gross Domestic Product per Capita," Federal Reserve Bank of St. Louis, last modified December 22, 2020, https://fred.stlouisfed.org/data/A939RX0Q048SBEA.txt.

6 Derek Thompson, "What in the World Is Causing the Retail Meltdown of 2017?," *Atlantic*, April 10, 2017, https://www.theatlantic.com/business/ archive/2017/04/retail-meltdown-of-2017/522384/.

7 Anne Case and Angus Deaton, "Mortality and Morbidity in the 21st Century" (conference draft), *Brookings Papers on Economic Activity*, March 23, 2017, 2.

8 Mother Teresa, "Mother Teresa Reflects on Working toward Peace" (essay), available at https://www.scu.edu/mcae/architects-of-peace/Teresa/essay.html.

9 Adam B. Lerner, "Poll: Republicans Say Obama More of an 'Imminent Threat' Than Putin," Politico, March 30, 2015, https://www.politico.com/ story/2015/03/poll-republicans-obama-imminent-threat-116503.

10 Celinda Lake et al., "New Poll Reveals Strong Bipartisan Support for Financial Regulation; Americans Say Wall Street's Influence in Washington Is Too High," Americans for Financial Reform, July 18, 2017, https://tinyurl.com/ y3mjgwqe.

## CHAPTER 2: RISING INCOME INEQUALITY

1 Emily Peck, "The 62 Richest People on Earth Now Hold as Much Wealth as the Poorest 3.5 Billion," *Huffington Post* January 17, 2016, https://www.huff post.com/entry/global-wealth-inequality_n_56991defe4b0ce4964242e09.

2 Barack Obama, "Remarks by the President at Howard University Commencement Ceremony" (transcript), Howard University, Washington, DC, May 7, 2016, available at https://tinyurl.com/y4t8zksp.

3 Michael Espinoza, interview series with author, April 28, 2020; April 30, 2020; May 28, 2020; June 25, 2020; and July 23, 2020. All subsequent quotations from Michael Espinoza are pulled from this interview series.

4 Alissa Davis and Lawrence Mishel, "CEO Pay Continues to Rise as Typical Workers Are Paid Less," Economic Policy Institute, June 12, 2014, https://www.epi.org/publication/ceo-pay-continues-to-rise/.

5 Rick Wartzman, "Open Letter to SEC Chairwoman Mary L. Shapiro," US Securities and Exchange Commission, February 17, 2011, available at https://www.sec.gov/comments/df-title-ix/executive-compensation/executive compensation-60.pdf.

6 Economic Policy Institute, "CEO Compensation and CEO-to-Worker Compensations Ratio, 1965–2011 (2011 Dollars)," The State of Working America, last modified June 18, 2012, http://www.stateofworkingamerica.org/chart/swa-wages-table-4-43-ceo-compensation-ceo/.

7 Sarah Anderson et al., "Executive Excess: CEO Pay and the Great Recession," Institute for Policy Studies, September 1, 2010, http://www.ips-dc.org/executive_excess_2010/.

8 Alexander Soule, "Pitney Bowes Shrinks Again—Barely," *Stamford Advocate*, February 23, 2016, https://www.stamfordadvocate.com/business/article/Pitney-Bowes-shrinks-again-barely-6849223.php.

9 "Pitney Bowes, Inc., Schedule 14A Notice of the 2016 Annual Meeting and Proxy Statement for Fiscal Year Ending December 31, 2015," EDGAR, Securities and Exchange Commission, 2016, p. 61, https://tinyurl.com/yapusy9d.

10 Robert Frank, "Jeff Bezos Is Now the Richest Man in Modern History," CNBC, July 16, 2018, https://www.cnbc.com/2018/07/16/jeff-bezos-is-now-the-richest-man-in-modern-history.html.

11 Dennis Green, "Data from States Shows Thousands of Amazon Employees Are on Food Stamps," *Business Insider*, August 25, 2018, https://www.business insider.com/amazon-employees-on-food-stamps-2018-8.

12 Piketty, Saez, and Zucman, *Distributional National Accounts*, p. 41, table 2.

13 Piketty, Saez, and Zucman, abstract.

14  Piketty, Saez, and Zucman, appendix, table B1.

15  Piketty, Saez, and Zucman, appendix, table B1.

16  Facundo Alvaredo et al., "World Inequality Report 2018," World Inequality Lab, accessed February 22, 2021, fig. E3, http://wir2018.wid.world/executive -summary.html.

17  Economic Policy Institute, "Average Family Income Growth, by Income Group, 1947–2013," The State of Working America, last modified September 25, 2014, http://www.stateofworkingamerica.org/chart/swa-income -figure-2c-average-family-income/.

18  Economic Policy Institute, "Change in Average Real Annual Household Income, by Income Group, 1979–2010," The State of Working America, accessed February 22, 2021, http://stateofworkingamerica.org/chart/swa -income-figure-2m-change-real-annual/.

19  Houston Peace and Justice Center, email to Michael Espinoza, June 13, 2012.

20  Laura Sullivan et al., *The Racial Wealth Gap, 2015*, 2015, p. 24, fig. 14, https:// www.demos.org/sites/default/files/publications/RacialWealthGap_2.pdf.

21  "Historical Income Tables: Income Inequality," US Census Bureau, last modified September 8, 2020, table H-3, https://tinyurl.com/y475wfar.

22  "The Simple Truth about the Gender Pay Gap: Fall 2018 Edition," AAUW, 2017, p. 5, https://www.aauw.org/app/uploads/2020/02/AAUW-2018-Simple Truth-nsa.pdf.

23  "Simple Truth."

## CHAPTER 3: RISING WEALTH INEQUALITY

1  Joanna Williams [alias], interview series with author, May 19, 2020; May 20, 2020; August 4, 2020; and August 10, 2020. All subsequent quotations from Joanna Williams are pulled from this interview series. To protect Joanna's identity, her name has been changed. All other details about her and her story remain accurate.

2  Edward N. Wolff, "Household Wealth Trends in the United States, 1962 to 2016: Has Middle Class Wealth Recovered?," NBER Working Paper No. 24085, November 2017, p. 44, table 2, https://www.nber.org/system/files/ working_papers/w24085/w24085.pdf.

3  Edward N. Wolff, "Change in Average Wealth, by Wealth Group, 1962–2010 (Thousands of 2010 Dollars)," The State of Working America, last modified August 10, 2012, http://www.stateofworkingamerica.org/chart/swa-wealth -table-6-3-change-average-wealth/.

4 Wolff.

5 Edward N. Wolff, "Ratio of Average Top 1% Household Wealth to Median Wealth, 1962–2010," The State of Working America, last modified August 20, 2012, http://www.stateofworkingamerica.org/chart/swa-wealth-figure-6c-ratio-top-1-wealth/index.html.

6 Edward N. Wolff, as cited in Christopher Ingraham, "The Richest 1 Percent Now Owns More of the Country's Wealth Than at Any Time in the Past 50 Years," Washington Post, December 6, 2017, https://tinyurl.com/y5f6m857.

7 Ingraham.

8 Emmanuel Saez and Gabriel Zucman, "Exploding wealth inequality in the United States," October 2014, https://live-equitablegrowth.pantheonsite.io/wp-content/uploads/2014/10/102014-wealth-brief.pdf.

9 "Urban Institute Calculations from Survey of Financial Characteristics of Consumers 1962 (December 31), Survey of Changes in Family Finances 1963, and Survey of Consumer Finances 1983–2016," Urban Institute, accessed February 24, 2021, chart 3, http://apps.urban.org/features/wealth-inequality-charts.

10 Chuck Collins and Josh Hoxie, "Income Inequality Is Bad Enough, Then Add the Race Factor," The Hill, November 21, 2017, https://tinyurl.com/yc4lwj2d.

11 Richard Rothstein, *The Color of Law: A Forgotten History of How Our Government Segregated America* (New York: Liveright, 2017), 186.

12 Laura Sullivan et al., "The Racial Wealth Gap: Why Policy Matters," Demos & Institute for Assets & Social Policy, Brandeis University, 2015, p. 1, https://www.demos.org/sites/default/files/publications/RacialWealthGap_2.pdf.

13 Rothstein, *Color of Law*.

14 Rothstein, 173.

15 Andrew Reschovsky, "The Future of U.S. Public School Revenue from the Property Tax," Lincoln Institute of Land and Policy, July 2017, https://tinyurl.com/y2t9fale.

16 *$23 Billion*, EdBuild, February 2019, https://edbuild.org/content/23-billion/full-report.pdf.

17 "State High School Graduation Rates by Race, Ethnicity," Governing: The Future of States of Localities, accessed April 27, 2021, https://www.governing.com/archive/state-high-school-graduation-rates-by-race-ethnicity.html.

18 Mikhail Zinshteyn, "College Graduation Rates Rise, but Racial Gaps Persist and Men Still Out-Earn Women," Hechinger Report, May 26, 2016, http://

hechingerreport.org/college-graduation-rates-rise-racial-gaps-persist-men
-still-earn-women/.

19  National Institute on Retirement Security, "Women 80 Percent More Likely
    Than Men to Be Impoverished in Retirement," press release, March 1,
    2016, https://www.nirsonline.org/2016/03/women-80-more-likely-to-be
    -impoverished-in-retirement/.

20  Diana Farrell and Karen Persichilli Keogh, "The Gender Wage Gap Gets
    a Lot of Attention, but Another Metric Is Even More Disconcerting," *Busi-
    ness Insider*, May 15, 2017, http://www.businessinsider.com/jpmorgan-on
    -gender-wealth-gap-2017-5.

## CHAPTER 4: WHY INCOME INEQUALITY IS RISING

1   Clete Kiley, interview series with author, April 22, 2020; April 30, 2020;
    May 22, 2020; and June 19, 2020. All subsequent quotations from Clete Kiley
    are pulled from this interview series.

2   Olivia B. Waxman, "The Surprising Story behind This Shocking Photo of
    Martin Luther King Jr. Under Attack," *Time*, last modified January 16, 2020,
    https://time.com/5096937/martin-luther-king-jr-picture-chicago/.

3   Katherine Yester, "Measuring Globalization," *Foreign Policy*, November 20,
    2009, http://foreignpolicy.com/2009/11/20/measuring-globalization/.

4   United Nations Conference on Trade and Development, *UNCTAD Training
    Manual on Statistics for FDI and the Operations of TNCs*, 2009, http://unctad.org/
    en/Docs/diaeia20092_en.pdf, 2:2.

5   Yester, "Measuring Globalization."

6   US Census Bureau statistics, cited in Lauren Carroll, "Trump: Since China
    Joined WTO, U.S. Has Lost 60,000 Factories," *PolitiFact*, March 24, 2017,
    https://tinyurl.com/y6nsbs79.

7   "Where American Jobs Went," *The Week*, March 18, 2011, https://theweek
    .com/articles/486362/where-americas-jobs-went/.

8   Steve Pearlstein, "Outsourcing: What's the True Impact? Counting Jobs Is Only
    Part of the Answer," *Washington Post*, July 1, 2012, https://tinyurl.com/y6zofwbq.

9   Gordon Hanson, Chen Liu, and Craig McIntosh, "The Rise and Fall of U.S.
    Low-Skilled Immigration," *Brookings Papers on Economic Activity*, Spring 2017,
    pp. 84, 97, https://gps.ucsd.edu/_files/faculty/hanson/hanson_publication
    _immigration_risefall.pdf.

10  Gianmarco Ottaviano, Giovanni Peri, and Greg C. Wright, *Immigration, Off-
    shoring, and American Jobs*, Center for Economic Performance (CEP) Discussion

Paper No. 1147, May 2012, http://cep.lse.ac.uk/pubs/download/dp1147 .pdf.

11 Gaetano Basso and Giovanni Peri, "The Association between Immigration and Labor Market Outcomes in the United States," Institute of Labor Economics (IZA) Discussion Paper No. 9436, 2015, https://ideas.repec.org/p/ iza/izadps/dp9436.html.

12 Mike Collins, "The Decline of Unions Is a Middle Class Problem," *Forbes*, March 19, 2015, https://tinyurl.com/y3hcahw9.

13 Megan Dunn and James Walker, *Union Membership in the United States*, US Bureau of Labor Statistics, September 2016, p. 2, https://tinyurl.com/y5gefegl.

14 Dunn and Walker, 4.

15 Ewan McGaughey, "Do Corporations Increase Inequality?," *TLI Think! Paper* 32, no. 2016 (November 30, 2015): 29, https://papers.ssrn.com/sol3/papers .cfm?abstract_id=2697188.

16 Colin Gordon, "Union Decline and Rising Inequality in Two Charts," Economic Policy Institute, June 5, 2012, fig. 2, https://www.epi.org/blog/union -decline-rising-inequality-charts/.

17 Dunn and Walker, *Union Membership*, 7.

18 Amanda Gosling and Thomas Lemieux, "Labor Market Reforms and Changes in Wage Inequality in the United Kingdom and the United States," in *Seeking a Premier Economy: The Economic Effects of British Economic Reforms, 1980– 2000*, ed. David Card, Richard Blundell, and Richard B. Freeman, 275–312 (Chicago: University of Chicago Press, 2004). Available as a PDF on the NBER website, posted June 2004, http://www.nber.org/chapters/c6750.

19 James Warren, "Press of Technology Stirs *Tribune* Strike," *Chicago Tribune*, July 21, 1985, https://tinyurl.com/y4gbjmtv.

20 James Warren, "3 Unions Strike *Tribune*," *Chicago Tribune*, July 19, 1985, https:// tinyurl.com/y4awpyvt.

21 James Warren, "Printers' Pact OKd by *Tribune*," *Chicago Tribune*, November 25, 1988, http://articles.chicagotribune.com/1988-11-25/news/8802190511_1 _printers-production-unions-annuity.

22 Angus Deaton, *The Great Escape: Health, Wealth, and the Origins of Inequality* (Princeton, NJ: Princeton University Press, 2015), 191–92.

23 "Unemployment Rates by Educational Attainment, October 2014," Bureau of Labor Statistics, November 12, 2014, https://www.bls.gov/opub/ted/ 2014/ted_20141112.htm.

24 "Median Weekly Earnings by Educational Attainment in 2014," Bureau of Labor Statistics, January 23, 2015, https://tinyurl.com/y9hp4sr9.

25  Carl Benedikt Frey and Michael A. Osborne, "The Future of Employment: How Susceptible Are Jobs to Computerisation?," September 17, 2013, p. 1, https://www.oxfordmartin.ox.ac.uk/downloads/academic/The_Future_of _Employment.pdf.

26  Michael Chui, James Manyika, and Mehdi Miremadi, "Four Fundamentals of Workplace Automation," *McKinsey Quarterly*, November 2015, https://tinyurl .com/y5nsov9y.

27  "Labor Force Participation Rate—Women," Federal Reserve Bank of St. Louis, last modified February 24, 2021, https://fred.stlouisfed.org/series/LNS11300002.

28  "Labor Force Participation Rate—Women."

29  "Labor Force Participation Rate—Women."

30  "Median Weekly Earnings."

31  "Parenting in America," Pew Research Center, December 17, 2015, http:// www.pewsocialtrends.org/2015/12/17/1-the-american-family-today/.

32  Jacob S. Hacker and Paul Pierson, "Winner-Take-All Politics: Public Policy, Political Organization, and the Precipitous Rise of Top Incomes in the United States," *Politics & Society* 38, no. 2 (January 29, 2015): 176.

33  Thomas Hungerford, "Corporate Tax Rates and Economic Growth since 1947," Economic Policy Institute, June 4, 2013, fig. B, http://www.epi.org/ publication/ib364-corporate-tax-rates-and-economic-growth/.

34  Registered lobbyist numbers come from "Lobbying Data Summary," Open Secrets, accessed February 24, 2021, https://www.opensecrets.org/federal -lobbying. Information on the corporate tax cut comes from Kelsey Snell, "Final Version of GOP Tax Bill Cuts Corporate Tax Rate to 21 Percent," NPR, December 15, 2017, https://tinyurl.com/y4jqlmcs.

35  "Politics Cost $200 Million: Record Sum Spent in 1964, Campaign Expert Says," *New York Times*, October 27, 1964, https://tinyurl.com/y4bxl7ru.

36  John Craig and David Madland, "How Campaign Contributions and Lobby-ing Can Lead to Inefficient Economic Policy," Center for American Progress, May 2, 2014, https://tinyurl.com/y2go7bgo.

37  Ryan Bolt, "John Oliver Breaks Down the Disturbing Truth of Congressio-nal Fundraising," *Newsweek*, April 4, 2016, https://www.newsweek.com/john -oliver-last-week-tonight-congressional-fundraising-443675.

38  Martin Armstrong, "The Mammoth Cost of US Elections in Context," Statista, July 28, 2016, https://www.statista.com/chart/5371/the-mammoth -cost-of-us-elections-in-context/.

39  "Top Statutory Personal Income Tax Rate and Top Marginal Tax Rates for Employees (2018)," Organisation for Economic Co-operation and

Development, last modified April 30, 2020, https://stats.oecd.org/Index .aspx?DataSetCode=TABLE_I7.

40  Thomas Piketty, Emmanuel Saez, and Stefanie Stantcheva, "Optimal Taxation of Top Labor Incomes: A Tale of Three Elasticities," NBER Working Paper No. 17616, November 2011, p. 43, http://www.nber.org/papers/ w17616.pdf.

41  Hacker and Pierson, "Winner-Take-All Politics," 170.

42  Jonathan Ponciano, "The Richest Hedge Fund Managers on the 2020 Forbes 400 List," *Forbes*, September 8, 2020, https://tinyurl.com/y3nngu9s.

43  Neil Wilson and Wilson Willis, "How the Hedge Fund Industry Has Evolved over the Last 25 Years," Alternative Investment Management Association, September 14, 2015, https://www.aima.org/article/last-25-years.html.

44  James Chen, "Hedge Fund," Investopedia, last modified October 27, 2020, https://www.investopedia.com/terms/h/hedgefund.asp.

## CHAPTER 5: ECONOMIC INEQUALITY
## PUTS PRESSURE ON EVERYDAY AMERICANS

1  Heather Boushey, speech at Vox Conversations conference, Washington, DC, April 27, 2017.

2  Jamaal Nelson, interview series with author, May 2, 2020; May 17, 2020; and June 14, 2020. All subsequent quotations from Jamaal Nelson are pulled from this interview series.

3  Bob Herbert, "In America; the 'A' Teams," *New York Times*, May 7, 1998, https://www.nytimes.com/1998/05/07/opinion/in-america-the-a-teams .html.

4  Rabah Kamal, Daniel McDermott, and Cynthia Cox, "How Has U.S. Spending on Healthcare Changed over Time," Peterson-KFF Health System Tracker, December 20, 2019, https://tinyurl.com/yy7hppas.

5  "100 Years of U.S. Consumer Spending," US Bureau of Labor Statistics, May 2006, p. 39, table 20, https://www.bls.gov/opub/100-years-of-u-s-consumer -spending.pdf.

6  "Consumer Expenditures in 2018," US Bureau of Labor Statistics, last modified May 2020, table B, https://www.bls.gov/opub/reports/consumer -expenditures/2018/home.htm.

7  "Consumer Expenditures in 1999," US Bureau of Labor Statistics, May 2001, table 1, https://www.bls.gov/cex/csxann99.pdf; "Consumer Expenditures in 2018," table 1.

8  Data on home prices come from the US Census Bureau and US Department of Housing and Urban Development, "Average Sales Price of Houses Sold for the United States (ASPUS)," Federal Reserve Bank of St. Louis, accessed November 25, 2020, https://fred.stlouisfed.org/series/ASPUS; data on median family income come from US Census Bureau, "Median Family Income in the United States (MEFAINUSA646N)," Federal Reserve Bank of St. Louis, accessed November 25, 2020, https://fred.stlouisfed.org/series/MEFAINUSA646N.

9  "Consumer Expenditures in 2018," table 1.

10  "Consumer Expenditures in 2018," table 1.

11  April Brayfield and Sandra L. Hofferth, "Balancing the Family Budget: Differences in Child Care Expenditures by Race/Ethnicity, Economic Status, and Family Structure," *Social Science Quarterly* 76, no. 1 (1995): 158–77.

12  Rasheed Malik, "Working Families Are Spending Big Money on Child Care," Center for American Progress, June 20, 2019, p. 2 https://tinyurl.com/yxwrvap7.

13  US Bureau of Economic Analysis, "Personal Saving Rate (PSAVERT)," Federal Reserve Bank of St. Louis, accessed November 25, 2020, https://fred.stlouisfed.org/series/PSAVERT.

14  Board of Governors of the Federal Reserve System, *Report on the Economic Well-Being of U.S. Households in 2017*, May 2018, p. 10, https://tinyurl.com/yclay38c.

15  Thomas Piketty, *Capital in the Twenty-First Century* (Cambridge, MA: Belknap Press of Harvard University Press, 2017), 747.

16  Piketty, 746.

## CHAPTER 6: ECONOMIC INEQUALITY POISONS OUR SOCIAL WELL-BEING

1  Richard Wilkinson and Kate Pickett, *The Spirit Level: Why Greater Equality Makes Societies Stronger* (New York: Bloomsbury, 2010), 7–9.

2  "Professors Richard Wilkinson and Kate Pickett, Authors of *The Spirit Level*, Reply to Critics," Equality Trust, accessed February 24, 2021, p. 17, https://www.equalitytrust.org.uk/sites/default/files/responses-to-all-critics.pdf.

3  Krista Tippett, interview with Michelle Alexander, On Being, April 21, 2016, https://onbeing.org/programs/michelle-alexander-who-we-want-to-become-beyond-the-new-jim-crow/.

4  "Criminal Justice Fact Sheet," NAACP, accessed February 24, 2021, http://www.naacp.org/criminal-justice-fact-sheet/.

5  Deaton, *Great Escape*, 82.

6  Deaton, 107.

7  Marian F. MacDorman and T. J. Mathews, *Behind International Rankings of Infant Mortality: How the United States Compares with Europe*, data brief no. 23 (Hyattsville, MD: Centers for Disease Control and Prevention, National Center for Health Statistics, 2009), fig. 1, available at https://www.cdc.gov/nchs/data/databriefs/db23.pdf.

8  Ashish P. Thakrar et al. "Child Mortality in the US and 19 OECD Comparator Nations: A 50-Year Time-Trend Analysis," *Health Affairs* 37, no. 1 (2018): 140–49, exhibit 2, https://www.healthaffairs.org/doi/pdf/10.1377/hlthaff.2017.0767.

9  "The World Mental Health Survey Initiative," Harvard Medical School, accessed February 24, 2021, https://www.hcp.med.harvard.edu/wmh/.

10  Organisation for Economic Co-operation and Development, *Obesity Update 2017*, accessed February 24, 2021, fig. 1, https://www.oecd.org/els/health-systems/Obesity-Update-2017.pdf.

11  Wilkinson and Pickett, *Spirit Level*, 83, fig. 6.5.

12  Samuel L. Dickman, David U. Himmelstein, and Steffie Woolhandler, "Inequality and the Health Care System in the USA," *Lancet* 389 (2017): 1431–1441, https://www.ncbi.nlm.nih.gov/pubmed/28402825.

13  Deaton, *Great Escape*, 66.

14  Wilkinson and Pickett, *Spirit Level*, 176.

15  Julia Belluz, "Inequality Isn't Just Unfair—It's Making People Sick," Vox, November 5, 2015, https://www.vox.com/2015/11/5/9675796/health-gap-marmot-social-inequality.

## CHAPTER 7: ECONOMIC INEQUALITY THREATENS OUR DEMOCRACY

1  Miles Corak, "Inequality from Generation to Generation: The United States in Comparison," unpublished article, p. 10, fig. 1, accessed February 24, 2021, https://tinyurl.com/y23ojafr.

2  Gregory Acs and Seth Zimmerman, "US Intergenerational Economic Mobility from 1984 to 2004: Trends and Implications," Economic Mobility Project, October 2008, 5, https://tinyurl.com/y5q3gs3j.

3  Susan K. Urahn et al., "Pursuing the American Dream: Economic Mobility across Generations," Pew Charitable Trust, July 2012, p. 3, https://www.pewtrusts.org/~/media/legacy/uploadedfiles/pcs_assets/2012/pursuingamericandreampdf.pdf.

4  Chase Peterson-Withorn, "From Rockefeller to Ford, See Forbes' 1918 Rank-ing of the Richest People in America," *Forbes*, September 19, 2017, https://tinyurl.com/yytngyzc.

5  Kerry Dolan, "The Definitive Ranking of the Wealthiest Americans in 2020," *Forbes*, accessed February 24, 2021, https://www.forbes.com/forbes-400/.

6  Les Christie, "Despite Signs of Broader Economic Recovery, Number of Fore-closure Filings Hit a Record High in the Third Quarter—a Sign the Plague Is Still Spreading," CNNMoney, October 15, 2009, https://money.cnn.com/2009/10/15/real_estate/foreclosure_crisis_deepens/.

7  Arne Kalleberg and Till M. Von Wachter, "The U.S. Labor Market during and after the Great Recession: Continuities and Transformations," *RSF: The Russell Sage Foundation Journal of the Social Sciences* 3, no. 3 (April 2017): 1.

8  Ylan Q. Mui, "Americans Saw Wealth Plummet 40 Percent from 2007 to 2010, Federal Reserve Says," *Washington Post*, June 11, 2012, https://tinyurl.com/y4cgxrds.

9  Alan Taylor, "Occupy Wall Street," *Atlantic*, September 30, 2011, https://www.theatlantic.com/photo/2011/09/occupy-wall-street/100159/.

10  Public Policy Polling "Voters Moving against Occupy Movement," press release, November 16, 2011, https://www.publicpolicypolling.com/wp-content/uploads/2017/09/PPP_Release_US_11161023.pdf.

11  Bernie Sanders, speech, January 5, 2016, transcript, MarketWatch, https://www.marketwatch.com/story/text-of-bernie-sanders-wall-street-and-economy-speech-2016-01-05.

12  Lisa Lerer and Julie Bykowicz, "Bankers Erect Fences to Deflect Attacks That Don't Come," *Bloomberg News*, September 6, 2012, https://tinyurl.com/y5ulr4lo.

13  "Confidence in Institutions," Gallup, accessed February 24, 2021, http://news.gallup.com/poll/1597/confidence-institutions.aspx.

14  "Government Gets Lower Ratings for Handling Health Care, Environment, Disaster Response," Pew Research Center, December 14, 2017, https://tinyurl.com/y2dqjnqn.

15  Mehdi Hasan, "Time to Kill the Zombie Argument: Another Study Shows Trump Won Because of Racial Anxieties—Not Economic Distress," Intercept, September 18, 2018, https://theintercept.com/2018/09/18/2016-election-race-class-trump/.

16  "American Rage: The Esquire/NBC News Survey," *Esquire*, January 3, 2016, https://www.esquire.com/news-politics/a40693/american-rage-nbc-survey/.

17  "Partisanship and Political Animosity in 2016," Pew Research Center, June 22, 2016, http://www.people-press.org/2016/06/22/partisanship-and-political -animosity-in-2016/.

18  "Partisanship and Political Animosity, 2016."

19  "Partisanship and Political Animosity in 2014," Pew Research Center, June 12, 2014, https://www.pewresearch.org/politics/2014/06/12/section-3 -political-polarization-and-personal-life/.

20  Frederick Solt, "Economic Inequality and Democratic Political Engagement," paper presented at the Midwest Political Science Association annual meeting, Chicago, IL, April 15–18, 2004, http://citeseerx.ist.psu.edu/viewdoc/down load?doi=10.1.1.601.9279&rep=rep1&type=pdf.

21  Drew Desilver, "In Past Elections, U.S. Trailed Most Developed Countries in Voter Turnout," Pew Research Center, November 3, 2020, https://tinyurl .com/y4738l3a.

## CHAPTER 8: ECONOMIC INEQUALITY ASSAULTS OUR VALUES

1  Ben Chin for Lewiston Mayor, "Stop Hate Rally on Main Street (Ben's Speech)," YouTube, uploaded October 19, 2015, https://www.youtube.com/ watch?v=IF0iuIzFFeQ.

2  Ben Chin, interview series with author, April 24, 2020; May 12, 2020; June 2, 2020; and July 28, 2020. All subsequent quotations from Ben Chin are pulled from this interview series.

3  Daniel Lippman, "Robert Macdonald, Maine Mayor, Tells Immigrants to 'Leave Your Culture at the Door,'" *Huffington Post*, September 27, 2012, https:// www.huffpost.com/entry/robert-macdonald-maine-mayor-immigrants -culture_n_1920630.

4  Robert E. Macdonald, "Enough Is Enough Coffee Breaks, an Unfettered Mob and America's Birthday," *Twin City Times*, July 5, 2016, https://tinyurl.com/y5ch7h37.

5  "Ben Chin Breaks State Fundraising Record in Race for Lewiston Mayor," *Maine Beacon*, September 1, 2015, https://mainebeacon.com/ben-chin -breaks-state-fundraising-record-in-race-for-lewiston-mayor/.

6  Ben Chin for Lewiston Mayor, "Ben Chin for Mayor: Campaign Launch," YouTube, uploaded March 5, 2015, https://www.youtube.com/watch?v=d _D2RRGKtYE.

7  Katharine Q. Seelye, "Robert A. Macdonald Wins 3rd Term as Mayor of Lewis- ton, Maine," *New York Times*, December 8, 2015, https://tinyurl.com/y2g4h7bb.

8  James Stuart Olson, *The Ethnic Dimension in American History* (New York: St. Martin's Press, 1979), 51, quoted in Vincent Parrillo, *Diversity in America* (New York: Routledge, 2016), 55. This chapter, through from another edition of the book, is available at https://www.sagepub.com/sites/default/files/upm-binaries/23122_Chapter_3.pdf.

9  Parrillo, *Diversity in America*, 47, fig. 3.2.

10  Parrillo, 49, fig. 3.3.

11  Peter H. Lindert and Jeffrey G. Williamson, *Unequal Gains: American Growth and Inequality since 1700* (Princeton, NJ: Princeton University Press, 2016), 38.

12  In the study of inequality, the Gini coefficient, developed by Italian economist Corrado Gini, rates equality on a scale where 0 is perfect equality and 1 is perfect inequality. Lindert and Williamson, 38, lists the Gini coefficients for the New England colonies in 1774 as 0.367 and for the Middle Colonies as 0.376. According to the Organisation for Economic Co-operation and Development, the Gini coefficient for the US in 2017 was 0.39. "Income Inequality," OECD, accessed February 25, 2021, https://doi.org/10.1787/459aa7f1-en.

While it is not necessary to understand more here, for those who are interested in diving a bit deeper, the Gini coefficient has been described by Angus Deaton as the "average difference in income between all pairs of people divided by twice the average income." Deaton, *Great Escape*, 187. For me, the best way to understand it is to look at a society with two people. If one person makes $100 and the other $0, the Gini coefficient is 1: the difference between the two is $100 divided by twice the mean ($50 × 2), which is 1. If both people make $50, the Gini coefficient is 0: the difference between the two is $0 divided by twice the mean ($50 × 2), which is 0. In the discussion of inequality among economists, the Gini coefficient is often what is used to define or measure the scale of inequality in a society.

13  David L. Ulin, "Common Sense That Changed the World," *Los Angeles Times*, July 4, 2005, https://tinyurl.com/y48qtdtn.

14  Frederick Douglass, "The Accumulation of Wealth," *Frederick Douglass' Paper*, November 28, 1856, available at https://jacobinmag.com/2020/02/frederick-douglass-accumulation-wealth-land-reformer.

15  Douglass.

16  Alexis de Tocqueville, *Democracy in America* (1831), trans. Henry Reeve, revised and corrected edition (1899; ASGRP / American Studies Programs at the University of Virginia, 1997), http://xroads.virginia.edu/~Hyper/DETOC/1_ch03.htm.

17  Tocqueville, chap. 3.

18  Ronald Reagan, "Remarks at the Presentation Ceremony for the Presidential Medal of Freedom," speech, January 19, 1989, available at https://www.reagan library.gov/research/speeches/011989b.

19  James S. Leamon, *Historic Lewiston: A Textile City in Transition* (Auburn, ME: Lewiston Historical Commission, 1976), 28, https://tinyurl.com/ y3r4bpr3.

20  Leamon, 43.

21  Scott Thistle, "Income Gap in Lewiston-Auburn among Widest in Nation, according to National Mayors' Group Report," *Bangor Daily News*, August 12, 2014, https://tinyurl.com/y32uynzn.

22  Deaton, *Great Escape*, 168.

## CHAPTER 9: WHAT WE OWN TOGETHER

1  Stephanie Morimoto, interview series with author, July 22, 2020; July 27, 2020; August 4, 2020; and August 5, 2020. All subsequent quotations from Stephanie Morimoto are pulled from this interview series.

2  Aimee Growth, "Entrepreneurs Don't Have a Special Gene for Risk—They Come from Families with Money," Quartz, July 17, 2015, https://tinyurl .com/y3pkcgol.

3  Peter Barnes, *With Liberty and Dividends for All: How to Save Our Middle Class When Jobs Don't Pay Enough* (San Francisco: Berrett-Koehler, 2014), 60.

4  Thomas Paine, *Agrarian Justice* (1797), available at http://www.xroads.virginia .edu/~Hyper/Paine/agrarian.html.

5  Frederick Douglass, "The Land Reformer," *Frederick Douglass' Paper*, August 15, 1856, available at https://jacobinmag.com/2020/02/frederick-douglass -accumulation-wealth-land-reformer.

6  LiveSmartVideos, "Elizabeth Warren on Debt Crisis, Fair Taxation," You-Tube, uploaded September 18, 2011, https://www.youtube.com/watch?v= htX2usfqMEs.

## CHAPTER 10: THE CITIZEN DIVIDEND

1  Suzanne Deffree, "Apple IPO Makes Instant Millionaires, December 12, 1980," EDN, December 12, 2019, https://www.edn.com/apple-ipo-makes -instant-millionaires-december-12-1980/.

2  "Global 500," *Fortune*, accessed February 25, 2021 https://fortune.com/ global500/.

3 Apple, "Apple Reports Third Quarter Results," press release, July 30, 2020, https://www.apple.com/newsroom/2020/07/apple-reports-third-quarter -results/; Apple, "Apple Reports Fourth Quarter Results," press release, October 29, 2020, https://www.apple.com/newsroom/2020/10/apple-reports -fourth-quarter-results/.

4 Barnes, *With Liberty and Dividends*, 41.

5 Larry DeWitt, "Research Notes & Special Studies by the Historian's Office: Research Note #3: Details of Ida May Fuller's Payroll Tax Contributions" (July 1996), Social Security Administration, accessed February 25, 2021, https://www.ssa.gov/history/idapayroll.html.

6 Emily Brandon, "What Is the Maximum Possible Social Security Benefit in 2020?," *US News & World Report*, July 7, 2020, https://tinyurl.com/y4d4xqqr.

7 "SOI Tax Stats—Integrated Business Data," Internal Revenue Service, accessed February 25, 2021, table 1, https://www.irs.gov/statistics/soi-tax -stats-integrated-business-data.

8 The median US household in 2015 was 2.54 people. "Current Population Survey, March and Annual Social and Economic Supplements," US Census Bureau, November 2019, table HH-4, https://www.census.gov/data/tables/ time-series/demo/families/households.html. The median household income in the US in 2015 was $55,775. Kirby G. Posey, *Household Income: 2015: American Community Survey Briefs*, US Census Bureau, September 2016, https://www .census.gov/content/dam/Census/library/publications/2016/acs/acsbr15 -02.pdf.

9 William Lazonick, "Profits without Prosperity," *Harvard Business Review*, September 2014, https://hbr.org/2014/09/profits-without-prosperity.

10 Barnes, *With Liberty and Dividends*, 41.

11 Sarah Kliff, "Why Obamacare Enrollees Voted for Trump," Vox, December 13, 2016, https://www.vox.com/science-and-health/2016/12/13/1384 8794/kentucky-obamacare-trump.

## CHAPTER 11: THE BENEFITS OF A CITIZEN DIVIDEND

1 Median rent in 2019 was estimated to be $1,097. American Community Survey, "Comparative Housing Characteristics" (tableID CP04), US Census Bureau, 2019, https://data.census.gov/cedsci/table?q=CP04&tid=ACSC P1Y2019.CP04&hidePreview=false.

2 The monthly cost of food at home for a family of four with young children is $889.40. "Official USDA Food Plans: Cost of Food at Home at Four Levels,

U.S. Average, December 2019," US Department of Agriculture, January 2020, https://fns-prod.azureedge.net/sites/default/files/media/file/Costof FoodDec2019.pdf.

3  "On average it costs $1,230 per month, or nearly $15,000 per year, to provide child care for an infant in a child care center in the United States." Simon Workman and Steven Jessen-Howard, "Understanding the True Cost of Child Care for Infants and Toddlers," Center for American Progress, November 15, 2018, https://tinyurl.com/y3f6m6ks.

4  Adrian D. Garcia, "Survey: Most Americans Wouldn't Cover a $1K Emergency with Savings," Bankrate, January 16, 2019, https://www.bankrate .com/banking/savings/financial-security-january-2019/.

5  Zaid Jilani, "Speaking to Corporate Execs, Larry Summers Mocks Opponents of Outsourcing as 'Luddites,'" Republic Report, February 6, 2012, https:// tinyurl.com/y558cuw8.

6  Carroll Doherty and Jocelyn Kiley, "Americans Have Become Much Less Positive about Tech Companies' Impact on the U.S.," Pew Research Center, July 29, 2019, https://tinyurl.com/y3d57kw9.

7  "Big Business," Gallup, accessed February 25, 2021, https://news.gallup .com/poll/5248/big-business.aspx.

8  Office of New York City Comptroller Scott M. Stringer, *Red Tape Commission Report: 60 Ways to Cut Red Tape and Help Small Businesses Grow*, July 2016, p. 6, https://comptroller.nyc.gov/wp-content/uploads/2016/07/RedTapeReport .pdf.

9  "Understanding Small Business in America," US Chamber of Commerce Foundation, 2016, https://www.uschamberfoundation.org/smallbizregs/.

10 Brad Hershbein, David Boddy, and Melissa S. Keaney, "Nearly 30 Percent of Workers in the U.S. Need a License to Perform Their Job: It Is Time to Examine Occupational Licensing Practices," Brookings, January 27, 2015, https:// tinyurl.com/yygdz4hw.

## CHAPTER 12: WHAT A CITIZEN DIVIDEND IS NOT

1  Danielle Kurtzleben, "Fact Check: Does the U.S. Have the Highest Corporate Tax Rate in the World?," NPR, August 7, 2017, https://tinyurl.com/ y6b7t5vb.

2  Organisation for Economic Co-operation and Development, *Corporate Tax Statistics, Second Edition*, 2020, p. 19, fig. 8, http://www.oecd.org/tax/tax-policy/ corporate-tax-statistics-second-edition.pdf.

3  "Episode 459: What Kind of Country" (transcript), *This American Life*, WBEZ, March 2, 2012, https://www.thisamericanlife.org/459/transcript.

4  Andy Stern with Lee Kravitz, *Raising the Floor: How a Universal Basic Income Can Renew Our Economy and Rebuild the American Dream* (New York: Public Affairs, 2016).

## CHAPTER 13: BUILDING OFF OTHER AMERICAN EXPERIMENTS

1  Jay Hammond, *Tales of Alaska's Bush Rat Governor: The Extraordinary Autobiography of Jay Hammond, Wilderness Guide and Reluctant Politician*, 2nd ed. (Fairbanks, AK: Epicenter Press, 1996).

2  Scott Goldsmith and Alexandra Hill, *Alaska's Economy and Population 1959–2020: Statewide and Regional Economic and Demographic Projections*, Alaska Department of Transportation and Public Facilities, March 1997, https://tinyurl.com/y3wxyu6s.

3  Hammond, *Tales of Alaska's Governor*, 150.

4  Alaska Permanent Fund Corporation, *An Alaskan's Guide to the Permanent Fund*, 12th ed., July 2009, p. 1, https://tinyurl.com/yx8pd2wk.

5  Mike Bradner and Tim Bradner, "The History of the PFD," *Frontiersman*, July 23, 2019, https://tinyurl.com/y5pxy8aj.

6  Sara Race, "Overview of the 2014 Dividend Calculation," Alaska Department of Revenue Permanent Fund Dividend Division, September 22, 2014, https://pfd.alaska.gov/LinkClick.aspx?fileticket=14A5gz0FKJA%3D&portalid=6.

7  Alex DeMarban, "This Year's Alaska Permanent Fund Dividend: $1,606," *Anchorage Daily News*, September 28, 2019, https://www.adn.com/alaska-news/2019/09/27/this-years-alaska-permanent-fund-dividend-1606/; Dylan Matthews, "Americans Have Fewer Kids Than They Say They Want. Alaska Has a Solution," Vox, February 7, 2020, https://www.vox.com/future-perfect/2020/2/7/21125303/alaska-basic-income-birth-rate-fertility.

8  Hammond, *Tales of Alaska's Governor*, 254.

9  Sarah Palin, interview by Sean Hannity (transcript), Fox News, September 17, 2008, https://www.presidency.ucsb.edu/documents/interview-with-sean-hannity-fox-news-part-1-2.

10  Kate McFarland, "Alaska, US: Survey Shows Support for Permanent Fund Dividend amid Continued Legal Controversy," Basic Income Earth Network, July 10, 2017, https://tinyurl.com/y43jmw2z.

11 "Eastern Band of Cherokee Indians in North Carolina," National Congress of American Indians, accessed February 25, 2021, https://tinyurl.com/yy6f7mmr.

12 Christopher Arris Oakley, "Indian Gaming and the Eastern Band of Cherokee Indians," *North Carolina Historical Review* 78, no. 2 (April 2001): 148.

13 Oakley, 153.

14 EBCI Treasury—Office of Budget & Finance, "December 2019 per Capita Announcement," Facebook, October 30, 2019, https://www.facebook.com/permalink.php?story_fbid=623980274673014&id=262756020795443; EBCI Treasury—Office of Budget & Finance, Facebook, May 1, 2019, https://www.facebook.com/permalink.php?story_fbid=520239178380458&id=262756020795443.

15 Richard Sneed, interview with author, August 22, 2020. All subsequent quotations from Richard Sneed are pulled from this interview.

16 Moises Velasquez-Manoff, "What Happens When the Poor Receive a Stipend?," *New York Times*, January 18, 2014, https://opinionator.blogs.nytimes.com/2014/01/18/what-happens-when-the-poor-receive-a-stipend/.

17 Parvati Singh et al., "Income Dividends and Subjective Survival in a Cherokee Indian Cohort: A Quasi-experiment," *Biodemography and Social Biology* 65, no. 2 (2019): 172–87, https://doi.org/10.1080/19485565.2020.1730155.

18 Linnea Feldman Emison, "The Promising Results of a Citywide Basic-Income Experiment," *New Yorker*, July 15, 2020, https://tinyurl.com/ycn7oy67.

19 Aisha Nyandoro, "Society Flourishes When We Invest in Our Most Vulnerable," TEDX Jackson, 2019, https://www.youtube.com/watch?v=NLzhRGRl2gw&feature=emb_title.

20 "How Is the $500 Impacting People?," SEED, 2017, https://seed.sworps.tennessee.edu/spending.html.

21 "The Magnolia Mother's Trust: Initial Pilot Report," Springboard to Opportunities, accessed February 25, 2021, is https://springboardto.org/wp-content/uploads/2021/03/Pilot-Evaluation-One-Pager.pdf. Last day accessed is March 31, 2021.

## CHAPTER 14: WHERE WE GO FROM HERE

1 In 1850, nearly 55 percent of America's labor force worked in agriculture. See Stanley Lebergott, "Labor Force and Employment, 1800–1960," in *Output, Employment, and Productivity in the United States after 1800*, ed. Dorothy S. Brady, 117–204 (New York: NBER, 1966), 119, table 2, https://www.nber.org/

system/files/chapters/c1567/c1567.pdf. By 2012, it was down to 1.5 percent. See US Bureau of Labor Statistics, "Percent of Employment in Agriculture in the United States (DISCONTINUED) (USAPEMANA)," Federal Reserve Bank of St. Louis, accessed December 2, 2020, https://fred.stlouisfed.org/series/USAPEMANA.

2 James Devitt, "Why Americans Resist Higher Taxes for the Wealthy," Futurity, September 8, 2017, https://www.futurity.org/progressive-taxation-equality -1537722-2/.

3 Mike Synar was one of the most upstanding and remarkable political leaders I have known. Elected to Congress at the age of twenty-eight, he served as a Democratic representative of Oklahoma's Second Congressional District for nearly twenty years. In 1994, the summer I worked for him, he saw the anti-Democratic wave sweeping his district and the country (which would eventually culminate in Republicans taking the House majority for the first time in forty years). Mike knew he was going to lose but was adamant that he not moderate the values that he held dear. By the end, he was so unpopular that he even lost his primary. Tom Coburn ended up winning Synar's seat and eventually moved on to become a US senator. Less than a year after he left office, Mike Synar died of a brain tumor at the age of forty-five.

4 Adam Clymer, Robert Pear, and Robin Toner, "The Health Care Debate: What Went Wrong? How the Health Care Campaign Collapsed—a Special Report," *New York Times*, August 29, 1994, https://tinyurl.com/y6fy35sb.

5 Jessie Hellman, "Poll: Slim Majority of Americans Support Single-Payer Health Care," The Hill, April 13, 2018, https://tinyurl.com/ycres6by.

6 Abdul Mohamud and Robin Whitburn, "Britain's Involvement with New World Slavery and the Transatlantic Slave Trade," British Library, June 21, 2018, https://tinyurl.com/y2wwpk8d.

7 "Liverpool Firsts," Liverpool History Society, accessed February 25, 2021, https://tinyurl.com/y4twkfjd.

8 Thomas Clarkson, *An Essay on the Slavery and Commerce of the Human Species, Particularly the African* (London: J. Phillips, 1786), https://tinyurl.com/y5rl49w2.

9 For a rich and detailed account of this movement, I recommend reading Adam Hochschild's *Bury the Chains: Prophets and Rebels in the Fight to Free an Empire's Slaves* (New York: Mariner, 2006).

10 "Historical Background and Development of Social Security," Social Security Administration, accessed February 25, 2021, https://www.ssa.gov/history/briefhistory3.html.

11  For more on these advancements, see Deaton, *Great Escape*.

12  "Historical Background, Development of SS."

13  "Historical Background, Development of SS."

14  *Report of the Committee on Economic Security*, Social Security Administration, January 15, 1935, https://www.ssa.gov/history/reports/ces5.html.

15  "Chronology," Social Security Administration, accessed February 25, 2021, https://www.ssa.gov/history/1930.html.

## ACKNOWLEDGMENTS

1  Krista Tippett, "Paulo Coelho: The Alchemy of Pilgrimage," On Being, August 14, 2014, https://onbeing.org/programs/paulo-coelho-the-alchemy-of-pilgrimage/.